ULTIMATE BASS FISHING LIBRARY

GUIDE TO
SOFT PLASTIC LURES

CHOOSING AND USING
GRUBS, MINNOWS AND OTHER CREATURES FOR BASS

MONTGOMERY, ALABAMA

INTRODUCTION
From obscurity to mainstream

BASS FISHERMEN ARE NOTORIOUS for tinkering around with lures. Some are better at it than others, and that is good news for anglers looking to improve their fishing skills. Two of the best in the trade are Bobby Garland and Herb Reed, both of whom can take credit for launching a renaissance of sorts in soft plastic lures.

Garland, at the time a lure inventor from the desert southwest (early '70s), one day poured melted plastic into a mold and out popped the Gitzit, a pinkie-finger-size-and-shape concoction featuring a hollow body with tentacles at the end. Garland created the breakthrough lure for fishing in the clear, deep impoundments of western states, like his native Arizona. Tubes have been winning tournaments ever since.

Next was Reed, whose innovative mind was awakened sometime in the mid-1980s after he watched bass after bass ignore schools of baitfish to attack injured or dying minnows. Reed eventually designed a lure that would capture the erratic behavior of a baitfish in trouble while concurrently capable of covering the entire water column. He also reasoned the predator instinct of a bass is immediately triggered by long, slender prey. The end result was the Slug-Go, which launched a category of baits that *Bassmaster* defined in 1987 as soft jerkbaits.

And then along came something that looked as if it crawled out of the Amazon jungle. The piece of plastic, with appendages of varying shapes and sizes sprouting from its body, had no real identity until *Bassmaster* once again defined it as a creature bait.

Creature baits, soft jerkbaits and tube lures all have one thing in common. In the package, they look as if they will not catch a fish at all. Removing them from the package, threading them on a hook and casting them into bass cover produces different results.

Because they come in literally hundreds of colors and myriad shapes and sizes, soft plastics require a systematic approach to achieve success. Some, like a grub, will work year-round. Others, like a lizard, work best in spring and fall. Learning the idiosyncrasies of the various forms of soft plastic baits takes hours of time on the water.

To put that element of time on the fast track, the editors at BASS have added *Guide to Soft Plastic Lures* to the *Ultimate Bass Fishing Library*. Lure inventors like Garland and Reed are among the many experts who share their wisdom in the following pages that are filled with detailed illustrations and chapters designed to make you a better angler.

And who knows. After pouring over the pages and absorbing the timely information, you might join the likes of Garland and Reed.

Copyright 2004 by BASS

Published in 2004 by BASS
5845 Carmichael Road
Montgomery, AL 36117

Editor In Chief:
Dave Precht

Editor:
James Hall

Managing Editor:
Craig Lamb

Assistant Editor:
Althea Goodyear

Art Director:
Rick Reed

Art Coordinator:
Leah Cochrane

Designers:
Laurie Willis, Nancy Lavender,
Bill Gantt

Illustrators:
Chris Armstrong, Shannon Barnes,
Lenny McPherson

Photography Manager:
Gerald Crawford

Contributing Writers:
Wade Bourne, Russell Browder,
William Dale Harrison, David Hart,
Mark Hicks, Bruce Ingram,
Michael Jones, Steve Price, Louie Stout,
Tim Tucker, Don Wirth

Contributing Photographers:
George Barnett, Charles Beck,
Darl Black, Wade Bourne,
Russell Browder, Paul Cañada, Soc Clay,
Gerald Crawford, William Dale Harrison,
David Hart, Mark Hicks, Bruce Ingram,
Michael Jones, Bill Lindner, John Phillips,
Steve Price, Louie Stout,
Gary Tramontina, Tim Tucker, Don Wirth

Copy Editors:
Laura Harris, Debbie Salter

Manufacturing Manager:
Bill Holmes

Marketing:
Betsy B. Peters

**Vice President &
General Manager, BASS:**
Dean Kessel

Printed on American paper by
RR Donnelley

ISBN 1-890280-09-7

SOFT PLASTICS are available in every conceivable color and in just about every imaginable shape. Learn how these versatile baits catch every black bass species in the United States.

CONTENTS

GUIDE TO SOFT PLASTIC LURES

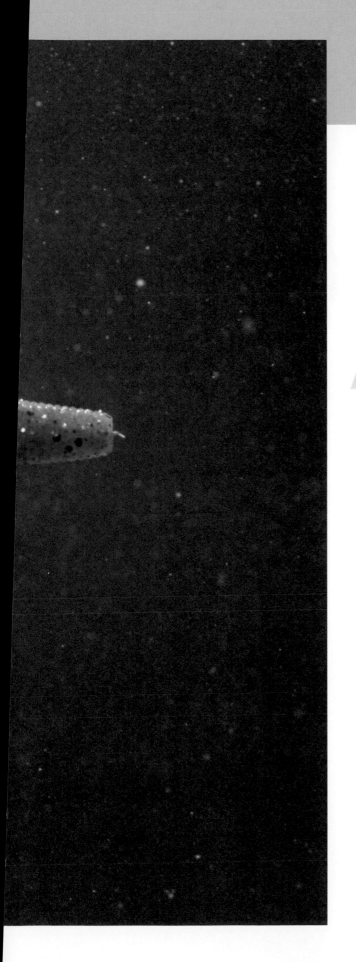

ALL ABOUT
SOFT PLASTICS

Sorting through the myriad of choices …

THE ELONGATED shape of the venerable plastic worm makes it the best soft plastic bait for slipping through dense vegetation and into the strike zone.

SOFT PLASTICS: JUST THE BASICS

Hot lures come and go, but these pros have made millions by sticking to the basics

TWO GUYS. TWO OPINIONS. And if you didn't know any better, you might think it was idle dock talk among a duo of bass fishing curmudgeons reminiscing about the good old days — guys who somehow stopped their growth as fishermen about 1975.

However, the truth is that Shaw Grigsby and Larry Nixon both share very similar beliefs about the power of "sticking to the basics." To these superstar professionals, the only really significant change in bass fishing has been the apparent willingness of many anglers to forsake the "old" in a headlong pursuit of the "new."

"The only real trends in bass fishing are the things being overlooked," observes Nixon, the 1983 BASS world champion and four time BASS MegaBucks winner.

"Take the old Texas rigged, straight-tail worm, for instance. Everyone is into Carolina rigging and doing different things these days, but some of the old standbys are standbys for a reason."

Rounding out the twosome is Shaw Grigsby, a member of the elite "Millionaire's Club" of the BASS pro tour with three decades of competitive experience, and growing.

"There are so many new lures, I think some people get caught up in the newness of things or the hottest new bait. When it comes right down to it, the old reliables tend to catch all the fish. Occasionally, a bait will come along — as the Slug-Go did years ago — that just wears them out. And it doesn't matter where you fish it. But that doesn't happen very often. Most baits are a lot of hype."

The first question any bass angler might ask is, "How can professional fishermen, paid by sponsors to promote their products, be so traditional in their thinking?"

Well, it's not because they close their minds to new ideas, they're just more cautious in adopting

(Opposite page) LEGENDARY BASS pro Larry Nixon makes his soft plastic lure selection based on prevailing conditions and cover. In the latter case, he believes it's not the cover or structure you're fishing that's key, it's how the bass are relating to it.

Soft Plastic Tip

Soft stickworms are deadly when fished wacky style, with an exposed hook through the middle, but they're notorious for tearing up. For longer life, cut a section of a tube lure and slide it over the worm, then slip the hook under the tube.

In choosing plastics, perhaps no other part of the equation gets more attention than color selection, especially among novice anglers. In the West, it can become even more difficult since this is the one area of the country that supports a very active and highly competitive group of hand-poured plastic manufacturers.

Although larger companies are now attempting to duplicate hand-pour colors, it is still something of an uphill climb. These subtle hues are sometimes quite artistic and only add to the already mountain of choices.

The way a professional avoids the "color trap" is simply by fishing different waters and observing his successes or failures and those of anglers he competes against. It doesn't take long to figure out that color is only one small part of the program. And, learning to limit those choices is unquestionably the mark of an experienced angler.

However, one area where bass anglers have strayed is in their use of traditional Texas rigged plastic worms. In many cases it's justified, especially since the new crop of plastic baits not only address

specific situations, but often do a better job than Texas rigged worms.

The danger comes in getting too far away from Texas rigged worms and not recognizing their inherent strengths. Whether you're doodling a 4-inch straight-tail worm in a clear, western impoundment or casting a 10-inch Power Worm to shallow structure in Arkansas, the venerable plastic worm is still a highly effective tool.

WHETHER USED independently or in concert with a hard bait (like a jig trailer), soft plastic lures add realism to a presentation.

On The Fringe Of The Limelight

It would be unfair to overlook other plastics that found their niche in the bass fishing art, but never generated a national buzz. While Jack Chancellor actually gave credence to the finesse revolution by winning the 1985 Bassmaster Classic on his French-fry-style, Do-Nothing worm, he did it with a Carolina rig.

At the time, this "bubba" version of the California split shot rig was just gaining converts among recreational anglers, and the true value of Chancellor's unremarkable Do-Nothing worm was somehow lost in the shuffle. Yes, the centipede and French fry worms to come would carve out a dedicated following, but not without time and promotion.

Even as the Do-Nothing-style worm built a following, the Carolina rig went by it like Jeff Gordon's Chevrolet. This time it was the method that really spurred the madness following a Classic victory. From that point on, Carolina rigging began to eclipse the venerable Texas rig in the hearts and minds of bass anglers with every type of plastic being tried behind leader, swivel and sinker.

Emerging from this whirlwind of interest was a plastic bait that had long been pigeonholed in a very specific, seasonal niche. The so-called "spring lizard" suddenly breathed new life with the emergence of the Carolina rig, and no longer were anglers bound by the lizard's unfair and inaccurate tag. Now, the scuttling, active nature of this plastic bait could be appreciated and put to good use.

RIGGING
SOFT PLASTICS

Add weight or go weightless —
either way you can't go wrong …

THE RIGHT RIG FOR SOFT PLASTICS

How you rig a soft plastic lure can determine how effectively the bait performs

IN TODAY'S FAST-PACED WORLD of bass fishing, no serious angler would limit himself to a handful of lures or a single rod and reel. And no bass enthusiast worth his flipping stick should fall into the trap of fishing soft plastics just one or two ways.

The most successful tournament pros, guides and weekend fishermen pride themselves on being versatile. That includes taking advantage of the various rigging methods of soft plastic creatures of all types, to match certain situations.

"There are so many ways to fish soft plastics," adds Florida pro Shaw Grigsby. "All have their time and place.

"You've got Texas rigs, Carolina rigs and the drop shot rig, which is very important now. And you need to know something about split shotting and the Mojo rig, which are really variations of the Carolina rig. Then you've got the floating rigs, where you tie the line straight to the hook or a little swivel. And you can't forget jigheads.

"In most situations you're fishing, one or more of these rigs will work. But in what situations do you choose one, and which rig do you choose? Generally, if I'm fishing weedy environments where there is a lot of vegetation, I'm going to choose a Texas rig or a weightless-type rig that works well in those conditions — where you don't get it hung in the weeds. If you've got a lot of weeds and throw a Carolina rig, Carolina rigs generally involve using a heavy weight, which will get in the grass and hang up a lot. Texas rigs can work in a wide variety of situations — from swimming it in shallow water, to jigging it in deep water. Because it's weedless, you can fish it in grass, brush and all kinds of cover.

"The drop shot rig is one I use a lot in vertical presentations, and I use it in relatively deep water. I'm not going to say you can't drop shot some shallow stuff, but basically, you'd want to use it in a 15- to 20-foot or deeper range. It's more of a vertical presentation. But it's one that's very finesse-oriented and an excellent, excellent presentation for clear water.

"When you're looking at split shotting, that's more of a light-line, finesse situation, while the Mojo is

(Opposite page) ACCORDING TO Shaw Grigsby, knowing when and where to apply each rigging method is the key to consistently catching bass.

Soft Plastic Tip

Drop shotting has become the most important new bass technique of the 21st Century. To master it, devote an entire day (more, if necessary) to fishing nothing but drop shots. Use a variety of lures, including minnows, tubes and finesse worms. You'll hook more fish by running an exposed hook through the nose of a lure.

more of a brush or rock situation to keep from hanging up. I use the floating rigs a lot in clear water, with brightly colored baits. A lot of times, I use a floating rig just across mats of vegetation."

Knowing when and where to apply each rigging method is the key to consistently catching bass in every corner of the country.

BEING DISCREET

In recent years, several rigging techniques have become popular. And all have the same basic theme — finesse fishing.

The drop shot rig: Born in Japan as the ultimate light-line finesse technique to counter the heavily pressured bass populations in their lakes, California fishermen quickly mastered the rig and refined drop shotting to get more productivity and versatility from it. As a result, the drop shot rig has proved its worthiness under a variety of conditions and situations.

"Drop shotting is very effective in places where there's a lot of fishing pressure and the bass see a lot of baits," says Aaron Martens, the California whiz kid who won several national tournaments on the rig. "It's finesse fishing at its best."

It is really quite a simple concept and technique. The drop shot rig positions a small, soft plastic lure in prime position for feeding bass — a foot or more above the lake or river bottom. The hook is tied on the line with a Palomar knot, where the end of the line is looped back through the hook eye to keep it pegged in position on the main line (coming from the rod). The length of the tag end determines how far the lure is positioned off the bottom.

The traditional drop shot setup consists of a small finesse worm impaled on an exposed hook and positioned 6 inches to 2 feet above a weight that is tied to the end of the line and sits on the bottom. In the West, the typical drop shot rig includes 4- to 6-pound-test line, a No. 1 hook, a 2- to 4-inch finesse-type worm and a 3/16- to 1/2-ounce weight.

The technique has become so popular that specialized weights designed specifi-

THE MOJO weight is a long, slender piece of lead with round, blunted ends. When properly rigged, it can be used to cover large areas of cover, such as tapering points.

cally for drop shotting, called Bakudan weights, are being imported from Japan. This ball-shaped weight features a swivel-like line tie that reduces line twist. It also has a unique line clip that allows you to change the distance between your bait and the weight without retying.

Although the drop shot was designed for fishing deep structure with little cover, some pros, like Arizona's Ish Monroe, have found that the rig can be altered to work in some bad places for some of the biggest bass that swim.

Monroe's flipping/pitching drop shot setup involves substituting a (3/8- or 1/2-ounce) Big Poly In-Line Jig (with a Yum Big Claw trailer) instead of the usual weight that anchors the rig on the bottom. About 6 to 12 inches above the jig is a Seducer Reaper impaled on a 1/0 to 3/0 Owner hook. Instead of light line, the whole rig is made of 17-pound-test Silver Thread.

The split shot rig: Many fishermen have long used a split shot rig in situations where the drop shot shines. The split shot rig can be used from shallow to deep, and it is considerably easier to fashion.

It begins with 6- to 10-pound-test line tied to a No. 1 or No. 2 small diameter offset hook. For shallow situations, a single, rounded split shot weighing about 1/16 ounce is used, while two shot (about 1/8-ounce) are better-suited for 8 feet and deeper. Most anglers position the split shot anywhere from 8 to 24 inches above the lure — and higher for working it through grass and brush.

"Don't create casting problems for yourself by using a leader that's too long," adds Terry Baksay, a Connecticut pro and finesse expert. "If the leader

THE SPLIT shot rig is a productive tool for fishing vertical structure like concrete bridge pilings.

Pegging Plastics

Although aids for pegging soft plastics and screw-type bullet weights have been embraced by fishermen in recent years, Florida pro Shaw Grigsby prefers the simplest way of securing a sinker to his hook.

"I use a long, tapered wooden toothpick," he explains. "I slide it in the back end of the weight and cut it off at the base of the weight.

"I peg it before I tie my hook on. I put the weight on, peg it, slide the weight up the line already pegged, and that will cut a groove in the wood. Toothpicks are real soft wood, so this will hold it and yet it won't damage the line. And if it did damage the line where you pegged it, you can simply cut that off as your tag end when you tie your Palomar knot to tie your hook on. Then I'll slide that up the line, fold my line over, double it, tie a Palomar, and I'm ready to go fishing."

is too short, it affects the bait's freedom of movement and doesn't look quite as natural. Personally, I have found that a 10- to 18-inch leader works best most of the time."

The Mojo rig: This downsized version of the traditional Carolina rig utilizes a uniquely shaped California-made weight that is marketed under the Mojo brand name.

The Mojo weight is a long, slender piece of lead with round, blunted ends. It is pegged securely on the line a foot or two above the hook with a piece of rubber skirtlike material using a special Mojo tool (or a dental-floss threader used for dentures). Although these weights come in various sizes, the 1/4-ounce model (which is about 2 inches in length) is by far the most popular among the pros.

The finished product is a hybrid of the Carolina and split shot rigs, requiring no separate leader, swivel or beads, and knows few limitations when it comes to structure and/or cover. The ends of points, sandbars, rocky points, chunk-rock banks, riprap, bluffs, underwater humps, boat ramps and flats are all ideal for Mojo rigging.

FLOATERS

The most common of the weightless rigs is the floating worm. But soft jerkbaits, tubes and certain lizards can also be used.

"I rig a floating worm a lot of different ways," says Davy Hite, a past BASS world champion and season point winner. "I rig it either with an exposed hook or Texas style, depending on the cover. But I almost never rig the worm straight, because it doesn't have any action at all. I use a 3/0 Owner Rigging Hook, and I almost always kink the worm up a little bit on the hook. That gives the worm some twist as it comes through the water. I like that particular action."

Hite estimates that he rigs a floating worm with a No. 3 barrel swivel about 75 percent of the time. The swivel limits the amount of line twist that occurs as the bait darts from side to side during the retrieve (which can fatigue monofilament).

Since weightless rigs are fished on or near the surface, they are most effective in water with good clarity. Shallow flats with brush or vegetation are prime areas for floating rigs.

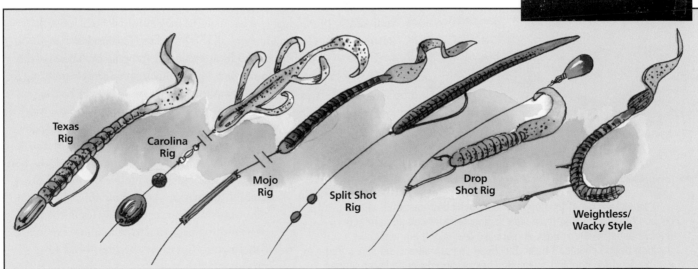

Texas Rig

Carolina Rig

Mojo Rig

Split Shot Rig

Drop Shot Rig

Weightless/ Wacky Style

ADD WEIGHT to a soft plastic rig when the bite is slow and bass are holding on the bottom.

GUIDE TO WEIGHTED PLASTICS

When times are tough, smart fishermen add weight to their plastics

BAITS THAT GO BUMP on the bottom and wriggle and writhe through the water have long been favored by Bassmasters.

Although their designs are endless, these baits are lumped under the category of "leadhead lures." Each features a molded metal head with a single hook. While some leadhead baits (jigs, for example) come ready to fish, others are sold as components, allowing the fisherman to rig his own jighead onto a separate soft plastic lure body (such as a grub, craw or shad) prior to use. Either way, savvy fishermen love leadhead lures because they get down to the business of catching bass quickly.

The term "leadhead" may someday be a misnomer. Environmental extremists continue to wage a war on the use of lead in fishing lures, and some tackle industry insiders foresee an eventual ban on the substance, with tin and metal used as alternative compounds. But no matter what material may eventually replace lead, chances are anglers will forever call this lure class "leadheads."

If you aren't proficient in leadhead fishing, you should be. These are the baits savvy Bassmasters should reach for when bass aren't actively prowling for food. Leadheads are for when bass are holding in weeds, stumps or on the bottom; when the water is cold and fish are sluggish; anytime the bite is slow."

The following overview will detail the conditions under which each should be used, the best retrieves, the most productive colors and other useful information. Hopefully this will clear up the confusion over leadhead styles in the minds of beginning bass anglers, and allow experienced fishermen to fine-tune their leadhead approaches.

(Opposite page) BAITFISH WILL oftentimes suspend along concrete bridge pilings, making a curled-tail grub a productive choice for covering the entire water column.

Soft Plastic Tip

The style of jighead used has a huge impact on how and where grubs will be most effective. Football heads are great for hopping over rocky bottoms; their shape causes the lure to wag from side to side. Darter head jigs are superb finesse baits; Western bass anglers like to shake them vertically through deep schools of bass. Ball head jigs are all-around styles that can be used for hopping, swimming or crawling down stairstep ledges.

GRUBS

The favorite leadhead lures of smallmouth anglers nationwide. Many noteworthy bronzeback catches, including Paul Beal's 10-pound, 8-ounce IGFA line class record, have been made on grubs. Experts use grubs in clear to slightly stained water with a temperature of at least 55 degrees (hair jigs often work better in colder water). Fish a 1/8- to 3/8-ounce grub with light line and a stout spinning rod, using either a drop or swimming retrieve. Start with a 4-inch grub body; switch to a 3 inch if the bite is light, or a 5 inch if the fish seem unusually aggressive. Curled-tail grubs are the gold standard for bass fishing, but don't overlook spear-tail grubs, especially for schooling bass.

Tip: Carry a good selection of grub colors with you. On sunny days, try clear or smoke with metalflake. On cloudy days or in dingy water, try chartreuse or pumpkin/pepper.

SHAD TAILS

These leadheads feature a soft plastic body that's shaped like a baitfish, with a blunt tail that catches the water, causing the lure to have a swimming motion upon retrieve. Shad tails with 1/4- to 1/2-ounce heads are perfect leadheads for current — the tail's action is maximized by moving water. Experts recommend the lightest line you can get away with when fishing shad tails in rivers or river-run reservoirs (lighter line creates less drag in current, reducing the "bow" effect and allowing you to detect strikes instantly). Use a stout spinning outfit when fishing shad bodies. They work well in virtually all water temperatures and clarities. Best colors mimic forage fish (pearl/black back, pearl/blue back, white); try chartreuse in muddy water.

Tip: Cast a shad tail upstream, hold your rod tip at 10 o'clock and allow the current to tumble the lure downstream along the bottom while reeling up slack to maintain a tight line. Set the hook hard when you detect a tap.

TUBE JIGS

Born in the deep, clear, canyon lakes of the West, these leadheads were among the first finesse lures. A hollow plastic tube with squid-like legs is pulled over a leadhead, so the bass feels only a spongy, lifelike sensation when inhaling the lure. Experts fish tube baits in ultraclear water on light line and spinning gear. Their slow, spiraling fall is like nothing else in the leadhead realm, and it works a special magic on bedding bass. Professional tournament anglers rely on tube jigs in early spring competition, sight fishing around pockets in grassbeds. Tube jigs typically employ lightweight leadheads — 1/16 ounce is common. (Some pros fish them Texas rigged with a slip sinker.) Popular colors include clear/flake, smoke, pumpkin/pepper and red/pepper.

Tip: When presenting a tube jig to a bedding bass, allow the lure to sit motionless on the bed, then make it quiver in place by squeezing the rod handle repeatedly.

THE QUIVERING tentacles of a tube jig are irresistible to bedding bass, which believe them to be predators.

Leadhead Mystique

Although many lure crazes have waxed and waned through the years, some form of leadhead is constantly at the cutting edge of bass fishing. Why?

Tampa, Fla., big bass expert Doug Hannon has an explanation: "Leadhead lures are the ultimate erratic baits, and erratic movement is the major key to realism in a bass lure. Look at a live crawfish crawling across a rocky bottom — it moves, stops, moves again. Bass connect stop-and-go movement with real food, and when you bump a leadhead craw or jig across the bottom, it exhibits nearly the same level of realism as the creature it represents."

Unfortunately, leadheads have a well-deserved reputation as "experts' lures." Beginners have the hardest time mastering them. Many have little built-in action of their own. Their attractiveness comes from contact with the bottom and with objects, as well as from subtle techniques the angler employs when fishing them. Anybody can reel in a spinnerbait and catch a bass; it requires a higher level of skill to work a jig or finesse worm properly.

SPIDER JIGS

These leadheads are known for catching lunker bass — both largemouth and smallmouth. They're bigger than most other leadheads and feature a plastic twin-tail trailer and an octopuslike circular collar positioned below the head. When a bass picks a spider jig off the bottom, the collar's tentacles wriggle and writhe inside its mouth, creating a lifelike, moving sensation. As a result, the bass will very seldom drop a spider jig, as is sometimes the case with other leadhead styles. Their weedless design makes spider jigs especially productive around grassbeds. Experts use 1/4- to 5/8-ounce spider jigs with stout baitcasting tackle and 14- to 20-pound mono or braided line. They work well in cool to warm water and are especially deadly when fished at night on ledges, humps or points.

Tip: Use only the reel's handle when retrieving a spider jig — not the rod tip. This lure's many appendages respond instantly to bottom contact and cause the bait to simulate a crawfish perfectly.

SOFT CRAWS

Leadheads with soft plastic crawfish bodies are especially productive in early spring, when real crawfish first emerge from their hidey-holes to crawl around rocks or newly

Quick Guide To Weighted Plastics

LURE TYPE	APPLICATIONS	COMMENTS
Grub	- Clear to stained water - 55 degrees + - Rocky lakes/rivers	* Use clear or smoke in clear water; switch to dark/glo colors in stained water
Tube Jig	- Clear water - 55 degrees + - Barren or grassy lakes	* Ideal for sight fishing to bedding bass
Shad Tail	- Clear to muddy water - 45 degrees + - Rivers/river-run lakes	* Let current carry lure downstream on tight line
Spider Jig	- Stained to murky water - 55 degrees + - Rocky/weedy lakes	* Use reel handle to move lure across bottom * Excellent at night
Finesse Worm	- Clear water - 50 degrees + - Barren lakes	* Use 4-pound line and translucent colors
Reaper	- Clear water - 50 degrees + - Barren lakes	* Use lightweight head * Pop lure off bottom
Soft Craw	- Stained to muddy water - 50 degrees + - Rocky/weedy lakes/streams	* Great stream lure * Use hot-colored claws in muddy conditions
Hellgrammite	- Clear to stained water - 50 degrees + - Rocky lakes/streams	* Crawl on bottom with reel handle

emerging weeds. Fish small craws on 1/8- or 1/4-ounce leadheads and larger ones on 3/8- to 1/2-ounce heads. Use a stout rod to "feel" them slowly across the bottom. The smallest versions are excellent baits for stream smallmouth. Soft craws are most effective in stained to muddy water. In low visibility conditions, use a craw with some hot coloration set against a muted background (example: brown body with chartreuse or hot-red claws). When equipped with a weedless head, a soft craw can be pitched or flipped in thick cover.

Tip: Live crawfish avoid light, so try soft craws at night and on overcast days.

FINESSE WORMS

Most anglers credit California bass hunters with inventing these slender bass-catchers, but the first true finesse worm was the Slider, the creation of Tennessee bass legend Charlie Brewer. Like other finesse worms that followed, it features a slender 4-inch, straight-tail worm rigged on a lightweight leadhead. Finesse worms are designed to elicit a strike when virtually no other lures can, and they are especially deadly in clear, coverless lakes. Their slender profile, small size and muted colors cause them to blend into the environment of the bass — the very essence of a finesse bait. Fish them on 1/16- or 1/8-ounce heads with a light action spinning rod and 4- or 6-pound line. Best retrieves include the "do-nothing" (simply cast, count the lure down to the desired depth and retrieve slowly and steadily without moving the rod tip), "doodling" or "shaking" (with lure head on bottom, gently shake the rod tip so the lure quivers in place), and "tapping" (use index finger to repeatedly tap the base of the rod while keeping the rod rock-steady, causing tip — and lure — to vibrate).

Tip: Under cold-front conditions or in a highly pressured lake, try "deadsticking" a finesse worm by lowering it to the bottom, reeling up a few inches and simply holding

WHEN GRUB fishing, the first cast is the most critical because the strike will likely come on the initial fall.

GRUB FISHING TACTICS

Designs, colors and rigging methods make the ages-old plastic grub an incredibly versatile lure

YOU KNOW THE PLASTIC GRUB.
The squat piece of plastic with the lively tail has been around for decades. Likely, your grandfather introduced you to the lure. Millions have been sold. Millions of bass have been caught on it — mostly little fish from clear, deep water.

You only thought you knew the grub.

This humble piece of plastic made a resurgence after falling by the wayside due to the influx of creature baits and other concoctions. Ironically, the grub benefited from the popularity contest of the new products and has once again become mainstream in the ever-expanding world of soft plastic baits. In the process, anglers have discovered that grubs are not just tools for deep or clear water. Instead, tournament pros have discovered its deadly allure in shallow water situations and some really bad places.

(Opposite page) KEN COOK prefers shad-type colors for grubs because the lures resemble the live baitfish.

"Grubs have become recognized as much more versatile in catching fish in a wider variety of places and conditions," says BASS veteran pro and former world champion Ken Cook. "Their popularity started out in deep water, but there's much more to fishing them.

"We've learned that you can Texas rig it on heavy line and put it in thick cover. You can fish it without a weight on top of grassbeds. And you can fish it so many other, different ways."

The qualities that make the grub such a productive lure in deep water also provide allure in shallow situations.

The short, fat body of a 2- to 5-inch grub resembles the bulky shape of several key varieties of

Soft Plastic Tip
Occasionally, even the most subtle of lures — leadhead grubs — are too animated for wary bass. When bass won't take a stock curled-tail grub, tone the lure down by slicing off part of the curl. The reduced tail action might be just what the fish demand.

Grub Fishing Tricks

Here are a few hints about fishing grubs from four of America's best grub fishermen:

■ **Gary Klein:** "With grub fishing, the presentation is critical. You have to make the first cast to a piece of structure as perfect as possible. The strike is most likely to come on the initial fall, often before you have even engaged the reel. And the strikes seem to come even faster in shallow water situations."

■ **Ken Cook:** "I mostly prefer shad-type colors, because I think that's what grubs usually represent. When fishing it like a topwater bait, I like brighter colors, like white or chartreuse-and-white, which allow me to keep visual contact as it crosses a grassbed. For most flipping and other cover applications, I prefer Tennessee shad, bluegill, smoke, and salt-and-pepper colors. In the darkest water, I use electric blue, plum or purple with a chartreuse tail."

■ **Joe Thomas:** "A 5-inch chartreuse-and-black metalflake Kalin grub is my No. 1 smallmouth lure. Fished on a 1/4-ounce jighead and 8-pound-test line, it's the perfect lure for catching smallmouth holding on rocky shelves and dropoffs at almost any depth. I let it reach the bottom and then snap my rod up. I then allow the grub to fall on 'controlled slack.' The smallmouth will almost always hit the grub on the fall."

baitfish. Crawled or hopped across the bottom, it can also closely imitate a crawfish. Its tail has a lifelike action and provides a tantalizing fluttering descent through the water. And the grub emits a surprising level of vibration that helps draw bass in heavy brush or grass.

Other reasons for the resurgence of the grub include advancements in color, texture and action available in modern soft plastic lures.

"Better colors — and more of them — and softer material have enabled us to develop new techniques for the bait and expand its usefulness," notes Cook.

Improvements in terminal tackle have played a major role in the new versatility of grubs, according to Arkansas pro Rob Kilby. He credits the development of the wide gap hook with helping make grubs more weedless.

"This hook enables us to Texas rig a grub for fishing cover, which is vital," Kilby says. "Until then, there wasn't such a thing as a wide gap hook."

The built-in qualities of the grub and recent technological enhancements have made it highly effective for catching pressured bass, even in shallow water.

Kilby's success in a Bassmaster Classic held on the James River is a prime example. Most of this third place weight came from casting a 4-inch smoke-colored grub around boat docks, duck blinds and pilings in the mouths of creeks. Despite heavy fishing pressure in those areas, he caught fish because, he believes, the bass had not seen any grubs.

Kilby is quick to point out that grubs and their terminal tackle must be suited to the water conditions. In murky water, for example, "there isn't a better color than silver flake," he declares. "And another key in dirty water is using a brass bullet weight with a glass bead between the weight and the hook." Pros call it "brass and glass." The clicking noise from the bead and the brass sinker, combined with the vibration of the grub itself, helps fish find the lure easily in dark water.

Cook, too, counts the grub as a standard flipping/pitching tool.

"I'll flip a grub throughout the year, because there are so many times when the baitfish are short and smaller than a plastic worm might imitate," he says. "A grub is not very long, yet it has quite a bit of bulk. It displaces enough water to help fish locate the bait, and its bulk and softness cause fish to hold on to it longer than other lures."

Most of the pros who flip or pitch a grub in shallow cover use a bullet weight and imbed the hook into the plastic, Texas style. The exception is three time Classic pro Joe Thomas of Ohio, who has enjoyed some outstanding days on weedy lakes like Tennessee's Nickajack and Chickamauga, using an unorthodox approach.

Thomas ties on a 3/32-ounce round jighead (often referred to as an "aspirin head"). The jig hook is a 3/0 Aberdeen, and it has a fiber weedguard.

"I don't know of anybody else using an aspirin head on a grub, but it is very effective around grass and milfoil," he explains. "With that weedguard, you can fish a grub in some thick places. The other key is that I like to downsize the whole package; I use a small 3-inch Kalin grub with 8-pound line on a small leadhead. When the fishing's tough, that subtle package will attract strikes from fish that normally wouldn't bite."

While Kilby somehow maneuvers a Texas rig grub through the middle of Lake Okeechobee's reed patches, others like working around the edges of weedbeds, partic-

THE DEVELOPMENT of the wide gap hook enables grubs to become more weedless, thereby expanding their coverage capabilities.

ularly under postfrontal, blue-bird skies.

"One of my favorite grub techniques involves using a big 6-inch grub as a topwater bait," Cook interjects. "Using no sinker, I Texas rig the grub on a big 5/0 or 6/0 offset hook. I fish it like you would a Slug-Go, except it doesn't have the darting action of a soft jerkbait. Instead, it has a spurting movement a lot like a buzzbait. You reel it across the surface and the flat-face piece of plastic sprays water, spits and sputters."

Another productive technique over shallow, thick grass is dragging it over the vegetation like a hollow-body plastic Rat lure, he says.

Lake Fork, Texas, guide Mark Stevenson is another big fan of grubbing in the grass. He and his clients catch scads of small bass in the fall — as many as 150 a day — by cranking a grub on a 3/16-ounce exposed-hook jighead along the edges of hydrilla beds. He also fishes grubs around boat docks, riprap and launch ramps.

When he spots bass chasing schooling shad near the surface, Stevenson loads a 4-inch Fat Grub onto a jighead and skips it across the top of the water to imitate an injured baitfish.

That's not really a new application for the grub, but fishing one in off-colored water is.

"A 5-inch grub can be just devastating in stained water, particularly those in colors like salt-and-pepper," Stevensen says. "In dirty water, the fish won't usually be very far down. They like to suspend in dirty water, about a foot off the bottom in 3 feet of water, for example. They won't be sitting on the bottom, so swimming a grub through them can be deadly."

Although there is a variety of ways to retrieve a plastic grub — from buzzing it across the surface to slowly crawling it along the bottom — Rob Kilby's standard method is the swimming retrieve. The technique has produced big bass in situations as diverse as shallow, bedding fish to those holding along middepth dropoffs.

In summer, Ken Cook often employs a Carolina rig to get the most out of the grub's allure. He rigs the bait Texas style, with the hook imbedded in the plastic to make it weedless, then ties it onto a leader attached to a swivel and a heavy slip sinker. In this rigging, the grub undulates above the lake bottom or cover and often entices a strike when a larger lizard or worm is ineffective.

Other rigging styles and applications are limited only by the angler's imagination. Maybe you'll find a few new ones yourself. A new day in the life of the plastic grub is dawning. And it's a good time to reintroduce yourself to this ages-old lure.

MOST PROS, like Rob Kilby, who flip or pitch a grub in shallow cover, rig the bait Texas style.

REAPERS ARE an ideal alternative
for fishing in vegetation because
they give the fish a different look.

REAPING THE BENEFITS

Spawned in the West, these finesse-style baits perform heavy-duty chores elsewhere in the nation

MOST OF THE ESTABLISHED BASS METHODS in use today were popular on a regional basis before achieving national prominence. The plastic tube is a prime example. Could the innocuous reaper be another?

A reaper looks like a narrow leaf with a short, fat stem — hardly spectacular. It was in vogue for several years with Midwestern and Western anglers who fish clear water impoundments with split shot rigs. Then its popularity spread to the East, where reapers gained converts in Ohio, of all places; a state where most bass are taken from stained, shallow water.

(Opposite page) JOHN SCHWARZEL fishes reaper-style plastics on a Carolina rig.

Instead of matching these lures with split shot and light spinning tackle, Ohio anglers combine 4-inch reapers with Carolina rigs sporting 1/2- to 1-ounce sinkers. It's a much faster presentation than split shotting and draws strikes from bass that are not in the mood for larger offerings. Smallmouth in Lake Erie's Western Basin can't leave them alone. Just ask John Schwarzel of Hockingsport, Ohio, who was introduced to the rig during a springtime bass tournament.

"I wasn't doing too well on my jigs and tubes," he recalls. "My partner was catching fish with reapers on a Carolina rig and was good enough to share them with me. We were working a ledge about 20 feet deep, and then I proceeded to put my limit in the boat in under an hour."

Since then, Schwarzel has duped countless smallmouth with the Carolina-style reaper. He also used it to catch good numbers of largemouth and spotted bass while on a fall outing to West Point Lake, Ga.

"I was fishing roadbeds and pond dams to

Soft Plastic Tip

Anglers are divided on whether the reaper imitates leeches, sculpin or other bass forage, but most agree that the baits work best when they're close to the bottom. Fish them on split shot or mojo rigs, where they're free to dart just above the dirt or rock and undulate slowly as they fall.

REAPERS ARE ideal for skipping beneath boat docks, due to their flat shape.

"You'd think that old fat thing wouldn't do much," he says, "but it looks exactly like a dying shad fluttering in the water. It's especially effective when you flop it back in brushpiles or any cover that lets you lay your line over something. Just pick it up, let it flutter down and work it in one place."

REAPING IT IN

While a jig-and-pork frog combination remains Chapman's No. 1 lure, the reaper frequently plays a cleanup role. He often seines a bank first with a jig and then works the same cover with a reaper. He claims the reaper takes fish that refuse the jig.

"I mean dropping it in the very same places," he says. "These fish just get wise to our baits. The reaper works because it gives them something a little bit different."

According to John Cassidy, a tournament angler from Del Mar, Calif., the reaper was originally designed for split shotting or Carolina rig fishing in the western waters that receive heavy fishing pressure.

"One key to this bait is its unusual action," he says. While most fishermen insert the hook perpendicular to the flat portion of the reaper, Cassidy says others do well by hooking it in the side.

The most popular setup, Cassidy learned, matches a 4-inch Texas rigged reaper with a 1/8-ounce slip sinker. The lure is usually pitched to cover with stiff spinning tackle.

A different reaper rigging works well for western pro Rich Tauber when he's confronted with especially tough fishing in western waters. He dresses a 1/8-ounce darter-head jig with a 3-inch Kalin's Salty Reaper and fishes it on 6-pound line.

"I use crawfish colors mostly, and I hop it over shallow, rocky areas. It gives you a supersmall crawfish imitation. I like pumpkin with green flake and other light, amber colors."

The reaper is gaining ground, but it remains a small player in the overall bass picture. The lure's banal appearance may be the reason it hasn't become more widely accepted with anglers across the country.

depths of 30 feet," he says. "The best structures had brush on them. I caught most of the bass by retrieving uphill, toward shallower water."

RIGGING THE REAPER

This hand-poured, floating bait features a thicker body than other reapers and accommodates larger hooks. Schwarzel has used Owner and Gamakatsu hooks as large as 4/0 with the 4-inch size. The lure also has an erratic action.

"If you give it a quick jerk," points out Schwarzel, "it raises up off the bottom and darts as it falls. I use lighter line with my Carolina rig to get a little more action; 8 pound for the leader and 12 pound on the rod."

Bill Chapman of Salt Rock, W.Va., one of the most successful bass tournament anglers in the Ohio Valley, may be the one responsible for introducing reapers to Lake Erie. On his best day with smallmouth there, Chapman and a friend boated over 200 pounds of bass, including several 4- and 5-pounders. He first got hooked on the bait while fishing shallow largemouth cover on the Ohio River, a subject he is reluctant to talk about.

These days, Chapman's edge is a 5-inch reaper rigged Texas style with a 3/0 or 4/0 hook turned and imbedded in the body, weighted with a pegged 3/16-ounce slip sinker. He flips and pitches a shad-color model to visible cover with a flipping rod and 20-pound-test line.

"This lure is commonly referred to as a do-nothing piece of plastic," says Cassidy. "The only thing we find that it does with any consistency is catch fish."

REAPING FROM TOP TO BOTTOM

While the vast majority of anglers fish these lures on bottom, some adventurous bass enthusiasts have found the flat design of the Reaper and its relatives perfectly suited for floating on top. Better yet, the light weight and flat composition provide for easy skipping under overhangs and docks.

In the vegetation-infested South, Tennessean Odell Braswell discovered the prime time for floating a reaper. During early spring, when the water level rises up into the trees, Braswell attaches the reaper — which he refers to as an eel — to 4-pound-test line and skips it under overhanging limbs and leaves. Braswell says the technique can pay off even when fishing pressure is excessive.

"That's when I win a lot of tournaments, when there are 200 boats on the water," he exclaimed. "I just cast and skip it back farther under the bushes, where the other folks aren't reaching."

Although floating traditional plastic worms is also quite popular, Braswell points out an advantage of the reaper's abbreviated size and compact design.

"It's super for floating. It works just like a worm — except fish that would just nip at the tail of a worm, will engulf the whole eel," he says.

To prepare the reaper for a surface presentation, Braswell threads 4-pound-test line through the bait with the assistance of a spinnerbait wire. He then runs the wire through the lure from back to front and attaches the line to the wire. A crimp on the end of the spinnerbait wire will hold the line in place while the line and wire are pulled back

Falling Reapers

On the fall of the bait is exactly where soft plastics specialist Larry Nixon found this style of lure to be most effective. He managed to capture and release two limits of bass in two days under heavy angling pressure on Lake Mead, using a version of the Reaper.

"It was one of those tournaments where we weren't catching a lot of bass," Nixon recalls. "We were fishing around a lot of boats, and it was tough to catch any quality fish."

But once he placed a leech imitation on his line, the reluctant fish suddenly turned bolder. Nixon set the bait up on 6-pound-test line with a 1/4-ounce split shot 10 inches above the lure.

"I fished it off bluffs 20 to 28 feet deep," he explained. "I cast it up on the bluff and then let it free-fall down to a shelf on the bluff. Then I would crawl it off the shelf and between the cracks, and the fish got real aggressive. They really wanted it.

"As soon as they would 'load up' and the line would get heavy, I'd start pulling," Nixon notes. "The fish really wanted it, and I knew if I gave them time, they would have had that thing swallowed before I set the hook."

through the bait. (Some anglers may prefer using a large-eye needle to perform this task.) Once the line has been run through the body, Braswell attaches a treble hook and buries the eye of the hook in the body, under the tail.

In addition to that rig, Braswell also enjoys attaching the reaper to the conventional leadhead and searching the weedbeds for bass hideouts. He has caught his share of elusive bass in the grass from Dale Hollow Lake in Tennessee and Kentucky. The veteran angler says the best method for fishing the weeds is to pull the boat right into the middle of the weedbed and cast in a radial pattern around the boat. Braswell recommends this technique on any clear, grassy lake — such as Dale Hollow, East Tennessee's Watts Bar or Alabama's Guntersville Lake.

Small-stream expert Jed Danielson prefers a Texas rig when scouring rivers and streams for bass. Danielson has also experienced subtle pickups when fishing the Jiggin' Eel, and he says patience is the key to a successful outing.

"They don't always take it right away," Danielson explained. "Many times they wait until it hits bottom, and then they look at it for a while. You move it just a little bit, and sooner or later they pick it up."

ANGLER ARACHNOPHOBIA

These soft plastics produce all year long

GUIDO AND DION HIBDON, the only father and son to have won bass fishing's world championship, don't wish ill on anybody. Their hearts go out to the many anglers who suffer the fisherman's strain of arachnophobia, the fear of spiders.

The sight of a spider sends arachnophobiacs into a panic typically accompanied by excessive sweating, rapid breathing, a racing heart rate, nausea and dizziness. Anglers' arachnophobia is brought on by soft plastic spider grubs. Though not as debilitating as regular arachnophobia, the anglers' version prevents afflicted persons from catching as many bass as they would like.

Most fishermen would rather be schizoid than deal with an empty livewell due to anglers' arachnophobia. If you suffer from this devastating condition, take heart. Techniques devised by psychiatrists can help you cope.

Visualization works wonders with some patients. Picture yourself in a bass boat on your favorite fishing hole. The sun is shining; the weather is perfect. You are fishing spider grubs and catching big bass on every cast. Close your eyes, soothe your mind, make it real. Feel better?

Some arachnophobiacs get over their fear by touching a live spider. Angling arachnophobiacs should try threading spider grubs on jigs, and even rigging the baits Texas style, if they can summon the courage. Be bold. Grab hold. Honest, they won't bite.

Therapy from experienced professionals is the best way to go. This is normally a costly proposition, but doctors Hibdon and Hibdon have generously volunteered their services. So lie down on the couch, relax, keep an open mind and let the healing begin.

"I fish a spider grub and a Baby Guido Bug nearly 50 percent of the time," says Dr. Guido. "I always have those baits tied on. If I see a bass, even

(Opposite page) WHEN FISHING rocky bottoms, Dion Hibdon uses a football-head jig without a weedguard with his spider grub. The football-shape head keeps the bait from getting snagged, and the exposed hook allows for a better hookup.

Soft Plastic Tip

They're called spider jigs, but these collared grubs with twin curled tails mimic crawfish more than anything else. Consequently, it's best to fish them on "standup" jigheads with flat or slightly rounded tops. When the jig touches bottom, the curled tails stand upright, like crawfish pincers.

THE ONLY TIME spider jig experts rig the lure Texas style is when flipping and pitching to heavy cover with stout line.

outside the spawning season, I'll fool around with those baits and lay a little bit of Hibdon on him."

The Baby Guido Bug, a lifelike crawfish imitation designed by Dion, has long been a staple bait for both Hibdons. The Hibdons have also been keen on the spider grub for some time. Guido claims his father, also named Guido, designed a bait similar to a spider jig decades ago. He tied jigs with short, living rubber skirts and threaded smoke and black flake Mister Twister Twintails onto the hook's shank. He dyed the tips of the tails green with Ritt Dye.

When Guido II started fishing tournaments, his father's concoction helped him pocket wads of cash, but he kept quiet about it. Legendary Western bass angler Bobby Garland introduced Guido to a commercially made spider grub at a tournament on Lake Mead years ago. Spider grubs have been part of Guido's arsenal ever since. What is it about the spider grub that generates such strong bass appeal?

"For one thing, the skirt is always moving," says Dion. "It flares when it hits bottom, and subtle rod movements make it come alive. The swimming curl-tails give the bait bulk and slow its fall. I think bass see it as a crawfish or a bluegill."

SWIMMING SPIDERS

In most instances, the Hibdons rig spider grubs on jigheads and fish them with bottom retrieves. But when bass are keying on bluegill, they often work spider grubs with a swimming retrieve.

For swimming presentations, Dion usually removes the rubber skirt from a 1/8- or 1/4-ounce Gambler Ninja Jig and dresses the hook with a spi-

der grub. He pitches this combination around boat docks and other visible cover, and works it with a pump-and-wind retrieve that never lets the jig sink deeper than 2 feet. A 7-foot, 3-inch pitching rod and 17- to 20-pound monofilament line puts the jig on target and extracts bass from tight spots.

"I got on a bluegill pattern at a major tournament in the month of September," says Dion. "It was at Cross Lake near Shreveport, La. I swam the jig through cypress knees and finished fifth."

The Hibdons go to the Ninja Jig any time they probe dense cover. They opt for the heavy-hook Ninja when flippin' and pitchin', and the light-hook Ninja when fishing with spinning tackle.

"The pointed nose on the Ninja comes through brush 10 times better than other jig designs," says Guido.

The Hibdons have so much confidence in spider grubs that they rarely use pork trailers. They even go with plastic in cold water.

"Most guys use pork when it's cold, and plastic when the water warms up," says Guido. "Well, we use plastic all year, and we have done so for a long, long time."

DION'S CLASSIC

Given their penchant for lure designing, it's no surprise the Hibdons devised their own spider grub, dubbed "Dion's Classic." The Classic is wider than other spider grubs, where the curl-tails join the body. It also narrows toward the head of the bait, which sports a lively skirt.

"Dad designed the Classic," says Dion. "Its flat, wide bottom really helps with skipping. A lot of spider grubs are too thin to hold a rattle. The Classic is wide enough to hold two glass rattles — one on each side of the hook."

Homemade 1/8- and 1/4-ounce ballhead jigs with bristle hookguards are bread-and-butter baits for the Hibdons when they fish with spinning tackle. They dress the hook with a Dion's Classic. Or, they pinch the skirt off a Classic and thread it onto the hook in front of a Baby Guido Bug.

"In the spring, we catch lots of bass on rocky

Jig Popping

When the Hibdons cast a Dion's Classic to a dock they know is barren of cover, they let the bait sink straight to the bottom, hop it a few times, crank in and make another cast. They work fast and efficiently, until the dock has been thoroughly dissected.

But if they know brush has been planted around the dock, they work the Classic out and probe the cover, as well. Guido claims he usually coaxes bass on brush to strike the Classic on the first or second hop. As with most Hibdon tactics, their hop has a special twist.

"Whenever we get on a piece of brush, we pull the jig up against a limb," says Guido. "Then we rip the rod tip up 2 feet to make the jig pop off the cover, and let it drop back. That sudden jump triggers the strike."

banks that have some brush on them," says Dion. "That's where the ballhead jig excels. It works great on rocks, but it's weedless enough to climb over a log or work through a brushpile."

Bare, rocky bottoms prompt the Hibdons to fix a Dion's Classic on a football-head jig. They fish a football head without a weedguard because it fends off rocks so well. They may go as light as a 1/8-ounce football-head jig when fishing shallow water, and as heavy as 1 ounce when fishing deep, especially in smallmouth waters.

"There ain't no finessing with smallmouth bass," says Guido. "Put on a 1-ounce football head with a Dion's Classic, cast that son of a gun out there with 17- or 20-pound Trilene XT, and start jerking and hopping close to the bottom. If you fish it slow, they won't mess with it."

About the only time the Hibdons rig Dion's Classic Texas style is when flippin' and pitchin' to heavy grass with stout line. They rig the Classic on a 3/0 HP hook and peg a bullet sinker to the head of the bait. Or, they spice things up with Gambler's Rat'Lin Florida Rig sinker, which features a screw lock. They prefer a 3/8-ounce sinker, but will use whatever size is needed to penetrate the vegetation, up to 3/4 ounce.

"Nothing will ever take the place of noise," says Guido. "When you combine Gambler's rattling sinker with two rattles in Dion's Classic, you'll call bass to the bait in heavy grass."

The 3/0 HP hook also comes into play when the Hibdons rig Dion's Classic Carolina style. They resort to this combination when bass turn off lizards.

"I also like a Carolina rigged Classic when I fish shallow water where bluegill are swimming," says Dion. "Any time bass are in water less than 5 feet deep, they're thinking about eating bluegill."

DOCKING UP

Nobody fishes boat docks better than the Hibdons. Their boat dock proficiency has come through for them in tournaments across the country. Depending on the dock, they use a light ballhead jig or a Ninja Jig — the latter when brushy cover is present.

"In clear water, where you have to finesse bass from docks, there are no better baits than Dion's Classic and a Baby Guido Bug," says Guido. "We pick docks apart with our jigs. We fish along every edge and shoot a jig into every crack and opening that a bait will fit in."

Most bass lie in the shade of a dock, points out Guido. While this is common knowledge, many anglers assume the shade is always beneath the dock. This isn't always the case.

"When the sun is low, there may not be any shade under the dock by the time the jig sinks to the bottom," says Guido. "Study the angle of the sun. The shade down on the bottom may be off to the side of the dock."

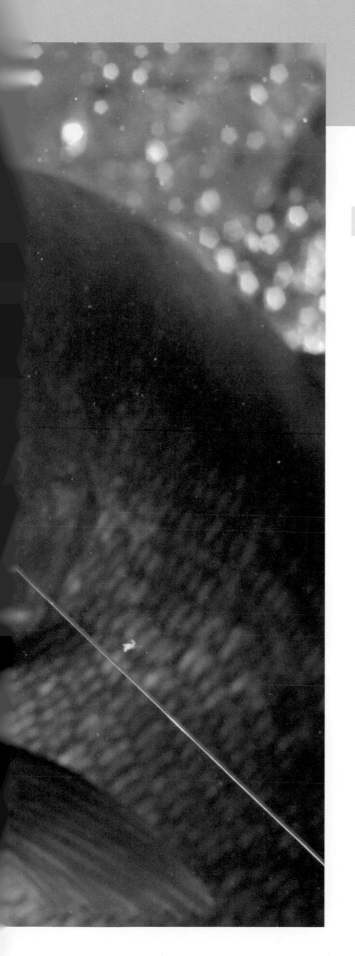

TUBING TECHNIQUES

How to skip, flip and pitch these versatile lures …

ESPECIALLY IN clear water, tube lures produce when other artificials fail to produce.

ULTIMATE GUIDE TO TUBES

Spring through fall, these tentacle-tailed tube baits are as effective as they are unusual

DENNY BRAUER'S 1998 Bassmaster Classic victory with a tube bait did more than give anglers another bait of choice for flipping heavy cover.
He gave the lure credibility and unshackled its inequitable reputation as a one-dimensional lure for finesse fishing junkies. Savvy bass anglers are experimenting with a variety of presentations, applications and methods for rigging these hollow, cylindrical, soft plastic lures.

(Opposite page) ART FERGUSON says tubes that fall straight, rather than those that spiral, are more effective.

Anglers are discovering that matching the presentation to seasonal patterns has much to do with how many bites the tube delivers. Here's a look at how successful anglers present their tubes during the primary bass seasons:

SPRING

There may not be a better lure for fishing northern waters soon after the ice leaves. That's when Ionia, Mich., angler Steve Gorham looks for cover along dropoffs and casts the tube at isolated cover on top of the ledge. He fishes the tube with a small jighead inserted inside the body.

"I let the bait sit on the bottom for a few seconds before giving it short, quick jerks to make it pop off the bottom," he describes. "When the fish are sluggish, I'm trying to keep the bait in the strike zone longer and trigger the reactionary strike."

Once the water warms and the fish begin roaming the flats, Gorham will look for shallower cover or drag the bait along the sandy or rocky areas of spawning flats.

The drag technique is the No. 1 fish catcher on the Great Lakes, where fishermen drift with the wind, and drag or swim tubes close to the rocky bottoms. The technique isn't recom-

Soft Plastic Tip
When Texas rigging plastic tubes, make sure to use a wide gap hook. The wider gap between the shaft and the hook point helps prevent the plastic from "wading up" on the hook point. Why is this important? Because the thick body of the bait needs room to compress when fish bite.

CHIP HARRISON looks for weedbeds growing near a dropoff because prespawn fish stage in such areas before moving to shallow spawning areas.

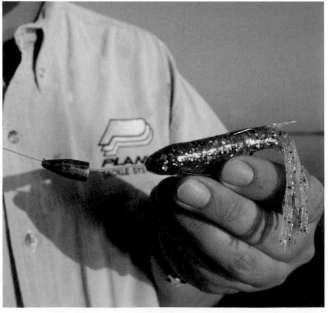

WHEN FISHING shallow water, opt for free-sliding sinkers on Texas rigged tubes, say the experts.

mended on lakes with a lot of grass or brush, but it's highly effective on expansive, hard bottom flats when you're searching for fish.

On lakes with distinctive dropoffs and weed edges, northern Indiana pro Chip Harrison looks for weedbeds growing near the dropoff — where prespawn fish often cruise before making the move to the bank. He lines up on the inside edge and makes long casts, popping the bait off the bottom in erratic movements. Like Gorham, he's trying to trigger reaction strikes.

"The action emulates a minnow or crawfish getting away," he explains. "It's the same principle that causes bass to bite crankbaits, except I'm doing it with a soft plastic lure. The fish reacts to the tube's sudden burst of movement."

Harrison induces the erratic movement by pumping the rod tip in continuous, short jerks. Although it may appear he is moving the lure substantially each time, he actually only pulls it a few inches.

"I accomplish that with a soft tipped, 7-foot rod and by utilizing the stretch in monofilament line," he explains. "By simply taking the slack out of the line each time I pump the rod, I'm not jerking the lure off the bottom; I'm only moving it forward rapidly so the fish don't get a good look at it."

The tube can be even better when bass go to the beds. That's when veteran BASS touring pro Shaw Grigsby is at his best, tossing the hollow plastics onto the polished bottoms in shallow water. The tube looks like a natural prey, and the bass don't want it in their nests.

"Some fish are more aggressive than others," says Grigsby. "I've found that you also have to experiment with colors until you find the one they'll hit."

Grigsby uses an Eagle Claw High Performance Hook with a wire clip that pinches onto the tube head to secure the hook to the plastic. Tiny lead weights with wire rings are inserted into the tube and attach to the hook.

If the beds have received a lot of fishing pressure, Greg Deatsman of Lake Odessa, Mich., opts for a modified split shot rig. He slides a small bullet sinker onto his line and ties a barrel swivel at the end before adding a 12- to 15-inch leader and a 1/0 or 2/0 hook. If there is a lot of cover, the tube is rigged weedless (Texas style); in open areas, the hook point is left exposed.

SUMMER

Tube flipping may be the hottest trend in fishing when bass are utilizing shallow cover. It's effective in the spring, but deadly in summer and fall.

"Jigs are still my favorite for flipping, but the tube bait is great for pitching into grass or behind other anglers who are using jigs," says Chad Brauer,

Tube Rigging Tricks

There are two basic ways to rig a tube: on a leadhead jig, or Texas style, with a worm hook and sinker. As a rule, anglers prefer the open jighead when fishing away from cover, and the Texas rig to make it weedless.

Here's how:

■ **Jigheads** — Jigheads are inserted through the hollow tail section and pushed up into the head of the tube.

Popular choices are the standard round ball head or the teardrop-shaped "tube" jig with the lead tapered on the hook. The latter will make the tube spiral more on the drop, but some pros prefer the round head, claiming the jig falls and swims straighter.

"I think it's important to keep the jig straight when it falls," says Lavonia, Mich., pro Art Ferguson. "There may be times when the fish want the bait spiraling, but the straight fall works best most of the time."

The angle and location of the line tie is equally important, says Indiana's Chip Harrison.

"If you're going to fish rocks or grass with an open jig hook, choose one that has the line tie coming off the front of the tube, not at 90 degrees," he explains. "The 90 degree line tie forces the tube head downward, and the eyelet catches on the cover. With the line tie out front, the bait pulls upward and is less apt to snag."

You can fish jigheads with wire or fiber weedguards, but rigging is a little more tricky. Rather than inserting the jig through the hollow end, you must thread the hook into the hollow body about 1/8 inch or more below the top, and then work it down into the cavity so the hook comes out of the bottom opening. Fold back the top of the tube and force the head of the jig inside the tube so only the weedguard is exposed.

■ **Texas rigging** — You can also rig tubes weedless with worm hooks by threading the lure onto a hook the same way you would a plastic worm.

However, worm hooks will tear through the plastic easily unless you're using a contemporary tube that has a thick, solid tip in the head. If the tube doesn't have a solid head, use a High Performance Hook with a wire clip that clamps onto the plastic and the hook eyelet to prevent it from sliding out of position.

For flipping big tubes into cover, some anglers use Gambler's screw-in sinker that locks onto the tube head and helps hold the hook in place. However, Denny and Chad Brauer prefer a traditional, free-sliding slip sinker in shallow water.

"Fish are less apt to throw the bait when the sinker is free of the hook," says Chad. "But if you're pitching a tube into grass or heavy brush, you need the sinker tight to the tube to help it penetrate the thick cover."

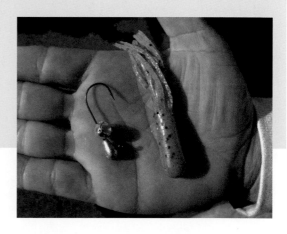

Denny's son and one of the rising stars on the BASS circuit. "Tubes are especially good when bass are keying on baitfish."

Most anglers opt for 4- and 5-inch tubes for flipping because the size and bulk creates more commotion when pitched into cover. Furthermore, bigger baits attract bigger fish. Lures are rigged Texas style, with a bullet sinker ahead of the bait.

"You can tie a tube onto a flipping rod and catch fish all through the warm weather months," says Grigsby. "It's also a good spring technique when bass are moving into bushes or spawning around cover."

Weed popping is a technique employed by Connecticut BASS touring pro Terry Baksay during the summer. He pitches a tube into pockets of weeds and "pops" the bait off bottom.

"You need to jerk hard to cause the bait to leap off the bottom," he says. "And when you're doing this, make sure you've got a rattle inside the bait. That helps the fish find the lure in the cover."

Harrison uses a similar technique for fishing deep flats.

"In most northern waters, you'll find a hard bottom shelf on the deep side of weed edges," he explains. "That's where perch spend their time in the summer, and perch are a favorite food of both largemouth and smallmouth bass. Best of all, most people don't fish out there.

"You can do the same thing along bluff banks of reservoirs," he says. "Choose shad colors and rig it on a jighead with a weedguard to protect it from hanging up."

Tubes also have found their way onto Carolina rigs, a technique veteran tubers have used for years, but one that is just now catching on with mainstream anglers.

"It's really effective on lakes with channels or ditches that are lined with cover," says Gorham. "The tube can be a better choice than traditional lures (like lizards) when the fish aren't as aggressive or want a more subtle presentation."

Enchance Tubes With These Tricks

Many pros believe a rattling tube is more effective when fishing stained water or heavy cover. You can attach rattles by using those that snap onto spinnerbait hooks, or stuff ball-shaped rattles into the tube cavity.

Steve Gorham of Ionia, Mich., prefers tiny tubular glass rattles, which he secures on jigheads below the lead. The rattles are held on the hook shank with electrical "shrink wrap," available in most hardware stores, that he slides over the rattle and hook. When heated with a match, the plastic shrinks against the hook.

Or, you can improvise like Greg Deatsman of Lake Odessa, Mich., did at Lake Erie one year when the water had been stirred by heavy wave action and he wanted to add sound to his tubes.

"My buddy and I went to a craft store and bought small jingle bells," he recalls. "I threaded the jig point through the hole in the top and bottom of the bell and slid it up the shank, then clamped them snugly with pliers. We went out the next day and caught more fish than the other anglers fishing around us."

Deatsman also adds flotation to his tubes when Carolina rigging or split shotting by stuffing small foam balls into the cavity.

"Poke them into the tube body before rigging the hook, then stuff a cotton ball up there to keep them from falling out," he describes.

Deatsman also packs the tube with scent, opting for "Smelly Jelly" because its gel-like composition stays with the tube longer.

"When fishing jigheads, I put a gob of the Jelly on a leadhead and slide it into the tube," he explains. "The Jelly releases slowly, and I think the scent makes the tube more appealing."

When rigging Carolina style, Gorham uses the High Performance hook with the clip. It holds the tube in place better than a traditional hook, he says.

FALL

Those summertime techniques are equally effective in the fall until the water turns cold. The fish are feeding heavily on baitfish, so the tube is a natural choice.

The difference is, says Deatsman, you may have to slow down your presentation as the water temperature plummets, but the fish may tell you otherwise. For example, if you notice that fish — especially smallmouth — are following the tube without striking, try speeding up the retrieve to trigger a reaction strike. That's when Deatsman prefers to sweep the rod abruptly to loop the bait high off the bottom and let it dart back.

"When the water gets really cold, you need to slow it down to a drag," he says. "The tube can be your very best choice in cold water, but the fish tend to want it moving slowly on the bottom."

That's yet another reason the tube bait is so versatile, say experts. Once you match the lure color and size to the forage, catching fish becomes a simple matter of determining the right speed to work it.

"Don't limit yourself to one presentation," adds Harrison. "The tube is much more versatile than most anglers realize, and a little imagination may give you an edge on those days when everything else fails."

Drop Shot Tube

When drop shotting, BASS pro Woo Daves nose-hooks a tube with a small drop shot hook and goes with a 24- to 30-inch leader. A lengthy leader allows for a longer fall.

"After the weight sinks to the bottom, I leave slack in the line until the tube touches down," says Daves. "Then I twitch and jiggle the tube back up. As soon as I feel the weight, I kill the tube and let it free-fall slowly back to the bottom. Bass can't stand that."

A long leader also serves well when Daves drop shots a tube next to shallow cover, such as a stump. He pitches past the stump and pulls the rig in until the tube holds adjacent to the cover, while the weight sits on bottom farther back. Any bass relating to the stump has a hard time resisting the jiggles and jostles Daves imparts to the tube.

THE OWNER Ultrahead has the weight attached to the head of the hook and can be rigged Texas style.

catch bass on a plastic crawfish virtually anytime. It truly is a versatile, highly productive lure."

The rocky geology of middle and eastern Tennessee makes the state's fisheries a haven for crawfish, and Hugh Harville is both a native and another expert on catching bass with fake crustaceans. Between the two experts, Murray and Harville can help you improve your skills at using this venerable soft plastic lure, a forerunner to today's "creature baits."

WHEN, WHERE TO CRAW

"There's not a bad time to fish a plastic crawfish," Murray declares. "You can catch bass on it from January to December. All you have to do is tailor your presentation to the time of year and prevailing conditions."

Murray follows simple guidelines for deciding which presentation to use.

"When the water temperature is rising after winter, I'll fish a jig-and-craw, pitching it around typical

EXPERTS claim that most plastic crawfish bites occur on the fall.

prespawn places: Deep banks running back in the creeks; treetops, logs, brush, rocks; docks close to channels, secondary ditches leading to spawning areas," he notes. "I'll fish any cover I see in less than 6 feet of water. If I keep rubbing the bark, I'll get a bite.

"After the water temperature climbs to 60 degrees, I assume the bass are spawning, and I'll switch to a Texas rig craw, or I'll use it as a trailer on a standard leadhead jig. I fish these around any type of cover on spawning banks and flats. Then, when the water climbs past 70 degrees, I'll change to a Carolina rig and work long points, bars, roadbeds and steeper banks close to the mouths of the creeks."

Murray emphasizes that if an angler is "getting his crawfish close to cover, he's in the right spot."

Harville says spring and fall are his favorite seasons for fishing a plastic craw.

BASS RELISH a meal of live crawfish, meaning it's important to make the fake bait mimic the real thing.

"I like to work banks that come off steep, especially if they're littered with rocks," he explains. "I don't know what it is about banks with softball-size chunk rocks on them, but they always seem to hold bass. I'd guess this is the right habitat for live crawfish, and this is where bass come to feed. Riprap banks fall into this category."

In summer, Harville Carolina rigs plastic crawfish

through patches of submerged milfoil. "This vegetation can be real good in hot weather, and it's a pattern most fishermen overlook," he says. "When you see milfoil matted on the surface, back out toward deeper water, and watch your depthfinder for clumps of grass that don't grow to the surface. Frequently, it'll only rise a couple of feet off bottom. You can Carolina rig this grass with a leader that's longer than the grass is tall, and this lets you skim that crawfish right over the top of the cover. This method can be extremely productive."

CRAW TACTICS

"If you just pull it through the water, a plastic crawfish has absolutely no action. It doesn't swim. It doesn't bubble. It doesn't do anything. So the fisherman has to add the action, and how well he does this determines his success with this lure," Harville explains.

He continues that a user must mimic the action of a real crawfish. "Sometime in their lives, most fishermen have turned over rocks in a creek and watched crawfish scoot away. They move in quick, short spurts and then run and stop, run and stop. This is what you have to imitate with a plastic craw.

"For instance, let's say you're casting a Texas rigged craw along a steep bank. After you cast, wait until it hits bottom, then pop it with your rod tip to get that quick movement like a real crawfish. You don't just lift and pull this bait like you would a plastic worm. You've got to impart that sudden little run of a foot to 18 inches. Then, when the craw hits bottom again, let it sit momentarily, then pop it again."

Harville continues that when using a Texas rigged plastic craw, it's imperative to watch the line at all times. "Most bites come when the bait's falling back toward bottom after you've popped it up. Sometimes you'll

Why Use Craws?

Crawfish guru Hugh Harville says there's one more good thing about fishing plastic crawfish: They will catch bass that won't bite other lures.

"I don't mind following other fishermen down a bank if they're not fishing plastic crawfish," he suggests. "If they're fishing spinnerbaits or crankbaits, they're probably fishing above most of the bass along that bank. I feel like I'll catch fish that they won't catch. Last year in a local tournament, my partner and I caught two 6-pounders off a bank that had just been fished by people in two other boats.

"For me, the plastic crawfish is the ultimate confidence bait, and it can be the same for others. If they can't catch fish on this, they might as well go to the house. But they've got to learn to fish it. This bait won't fish itself."

Two time BASS world champion Bobby Murray's parting advice provides a simple overview for fishing plastic crawfish. He offers, "Get it close to cover and close to the bottom. Then match your presentation to the season and prevailing conditions.

"So, it's sort of a co-op deal. If you do your part — use a plastic crawfish with the right methods at the right time in the right places — it'll do its part in providing strikes. Bass relish a meal of live crawfish. Make your plastic craw seem real, and it'll get eaten, too."

THE MOST popular plastic crawfish are 3 1/2 to 4 1/2 inches long and have pliable pincers that flap up in a defensive position when the bait thumps bottom.

PLASTIC CRAWFISH are meant to be fished on bottom, so maintaining close contact with cover is key to success.

feel these bites, and sometimes you won't. But if you're watching your line, you'll generally always see it jump and know you've got a pickup."

Harville employs several different strategies for using a Texas rigged craw. Most often, he works steep gravel/rock covered banks. "You go down a bank just like you're fishing it with a spinnerbait or crankbait, casting into the shallows and working it back deep. This isn't a slow method. Instead, it's fairly fast. If I'm in the back of a boat fishing a crawfish and my partner in front is fishing a spinnerbait, I can keep up with him. I just keep hopping the craw: Pop, pop, pop. Every time it hits bottom, I wait about a second, then pop it again."

Murray holds his rod sideways, with the tip almost touching the water when retrieving a Carolina rigged craw. Then he moves the bait with little jerks, allowing the bait to rest one or two seconds between spurts.

"Keep your sinker on bottom, and scoot it along instead of lifting it," he instructs. "You want to stir up mud or sand to attract the fish's attention. Then they see this crawfish scooting by, and wham!

"But let me emphasize that the key is making the movements quick, not lazy. Hold your rod tip within a foot of the water, don't allow any slack in your line, and keep pulling and reeling. This is a fast way to fish, and one that allows you to cover a lot of water."

Murray Carolina rigs with a big plastic craw on any conceivable deep structure from postspawn through summer. "I keep prospecting until I find some fish," he says. "I try points, humps, bars and other places where bass might be schooled. Usually, if I cover enough water, I'll find a concentration."

Flipping and pitching are other popular uses for plastic crawfish, and these are meant for dense cover like brush, buckbushes and vegetation. Harville prefers to move in close to such cover and flip vertically, while Murray likes to hold a few yards out and pitch to tight targets. The basic presentation is the same with both methods.

Harville frequently flips with a Texas rig crawfish rather than a jig-and-craw. He moves the bait quickly from one spot to the next, dropping the crawfish into a hole in brush or grass and letting it fall to the bottom. Next, he pumps it up and down a couple of times, lifting the rod 6 to 12 inches, then pulls the bait out and drops it in another hole. If a bass is there and feels like striking, it will usually do so immediately, he believes. So nothing is to be gained by leaving the bait in any spot

Craw Tackle

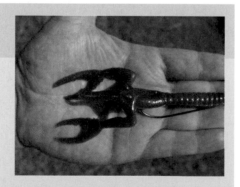

Hugh Harville and Bobby Murray use standard casting rods/reels for fishing plastic crawfish.

"My standard rod for Texas rigging is a 6-foot medium-heavy action casting rod. I'll match this with a fast retrieve reel and 20-pound-test line," Harville states. "For flipping, I use a regular 7-foot heavy action rod, and braided line in the 45-pound-strength class."

For Carolina rigging a plastic craw, Murray opts for a 7-foot medium/heavy popping rod with a straight cork handle. "I don't want a rod with a fast taper. Instead, I want one with a parabolic bend. This rod will have more give to it, and this matches up well with the Carolina rigging method of fishing." Murray Carolina rigs with 14- to 20-pound-test Silver Thread monofilament line.

Craw Rigs

Rigging plastic crawfish for their three primary uses is simple. Hugh Harville fishes a Texas rig craw most of the time. For that setup he uses a 1/4-ounce sliding bullet sinker to fish water up to 6 feet deep, and a 3/8-ounce sinker for greater depths. To stay ready to fish any depth, he keeps two rods rigged with one of each sinker size.

Harville rigs with a 4/0 or 5/0 Gamakatsu or Eagle Claw hook. A large hook offers more "bite" to penetrate a bass' bony jaw. He threads the craw onto the hook by inserting the point into the stem approximately 1/4 inch, then turning it and forcing it out on the belly side of the bait. Then the craw is slid up the hook's shank to the eye, and the point of the hook is turned and reinserted into the body.

"I push the point almost through the crawfish, but not quite," Harville instructs. "I like to barely feel the point when I rub a finger down the back of the bait. Rigging it like this gets the point out faster and allows for better hook sets.

"And last, I peg my crawfish with a flat toothpick pushed through the bait and the eye of the hook, then clipped off flush with the body."

Bobby Murray frequently Carolina rigs plastic crawfish, adding a 3/4- or 1-ounce weight and glass bead to the main line, tying on a barrel swivel, a leader and a 2/0 hook. The crawfish can be rigged weedless or with an exposed hook, depending on density of cover on the bottom.

When rigging a Big Claw on a jig, Murray normally pinches an inch off the crawfish's body. Then he threads the hook up and out the back of the bait so the bend and point are exposed.

FLIPPING AND pitching are ideal applications for plastic crawfish.

longer than a few seconds.

Murray normally pitches with a jig-and-craw, and he strives to make its entry as quiet as possible.

"I try to slide the bait into the water and drop it straight down," he says. "When the craw hits the surface, my rod is pointing at 12 o'clock. Then, as the bait sinks, I lower the rod to 9 o'clock. This allows the bait to fall vertically. If a bass hits the crawfish on the fall, it won't feel any resistance, so it's not alerted to anything unusual. On the other hand, I'll usually feel a thump, so I can lower my rod tip a little more, then set the hook.

"If there's no strike on the initial fall, I'll let the bait hit bottom, then lower my rod and snap the bait back up. This is a real slight movement. I don't pull the craw more than 6 inches off bottom, then I let it fall back in the same spot again. I repeat this procedure twice, then pull the bait out and drop it somewhere else."

MINICRAWS ARE meant to be fished in the toughest of all conditions.

ALLURE OF THE MINICRAW
Tiny plastic crawfish have become major factors in the pros' fishing success

P AST BASS WORLD CHAMPION and season points winner Guido Hibdon has long understood the appeal of small plastic crawfish on all species of bass.
The tiniest fake craws have quietly held a special place in the strategies of some of America's top tournament pros and guides.

Although minicraws are certainly a hit when fishing for spawning bass, they are by no means limited to that application. Small crawfish can be the ticket to overcoming pressured fish at any time, and they pay off handsomely in many other difficult circumstances.

"I learned a long time ago that baby crawfish drive bass wild," says Hibdon, whose favorite, the Baby Original, was designed by his son and fellow pro, Dion. "Years ago when I guided, I used to handpick all my (live) crawfish, and about 2 1/2 inches was without a doubt the deadliest size — especially for numbers of fish.

"That's why a small crawdad like the Baby Original is so good on pressured lakes. That's the very reason a baby crawfish works so well — it's the right size, and it's a little different than what everybody else is throwing."

(Opposite page) VETERAN FLORIDA BASS pro Bernie Schultz uses 4-inch craws in grass and stained water, but he switches to smaller lures for clear water.

Fellow world champion and title winner Mark Davis agrees. "If you get out in a lake and turn over rocks, you'll see that the average size of the crawfish is small — an inch to 3 inches long," he says. "The little plastic crawfish more closely imitates the food bass are used to biting. It's that simple."

Florida angler Tom Burke was baptized early in his life in the shallow, weedy lakes of his home state, where one of the mainstay techniques for home-grown anglers involves flipping a 4-inch minicraw.

"I've always thought smaller crawdads have a special appeal to bass because of their size," he

Soft Plastic Tip
When a tide turns and falls, bass often drop off shoreline flats and head to deeper water. Dock fish normally relocate to the deepest pilings they can find, or they even move offshore to ledges or humps. Also look for sailboats or yachts, because they require deep moorage, indicating there may be holes where bass will hold during the low tide.

allowing the bait to fall on a semislack line between tugs. When he finds bass holding tight to the bottom, he may also drag the lure like a Carolina rig. If fish are suspended a few feet above the bottom, he will get the bait up to their level before he starts pumping it.

NORTHERN KNOWLEDGE

"Up here, we don't have any shad," states Mark Zona, a Great Lakes-area guide and top regional tournament angler. But that doesn't seem to matter to the smallmouth bass he likes to chase.

Alewives, the Great Lakes' dominant baitfish, bear a remarkable resemblance to plastic shad baits. The same relationship also holds true for most of the other available forage, Zona believes.

He finds the baits extremely effective from pre-spawn through the spawn. "When the ice melts, bass stay on the edges of flats and on the inside turns of weedlines, where they feed on bluegill and minnows until the spawn," he says. In that situation, he mostly uses Bass Pro Shops' Squirmin' Shad in the 2-inch size and in bluegill or clear flake/black back colors.

Once the bass move to the banks, Zona shifts to sight fishing, often with plastic shad. "It is far and away the best sight bait I have ever used," he testifies. "I dye my lures either green pumpkin or watermelon, depending on water clarity. Green pumpkin works best on clear lakes, and anytime I'm sight fishing, I put some chartreuse somewhere on the body," he says.

During the spawn, Zona prefers a 3/16-ounce ballhead jig because he can make the lure rest at a nose-down angle by simply keeping tension on his line. Such a position, and the resultant subtle swaying of the bait, accurately imitates a small scavenger nibbling eggs from a bass' nest.

After the spawn, Zona switches to other baits until late summer, when the alewives vacate the main lake. "As the alewives come into the bays, smallmouth follow them. That's when I'll use pearl-colored plastic shad exclusively," Zona says, adding that alewives inhabit virtually all of the

The Seasonal Shad Bite

Although he has caught both large-mouth and smallmouth on them throughout the year, spring is Texas bass guide Jerry Taylor's favorite time to break out a bag of plastic shad.

"After the spawn, there are lots of little baitfish in the coves, and the bass will be chasing these newly hatched shad up shallow," Taylor said. "I like to fish gradual banks and grass edges where I see schools of small minnows. I stay back from the fish, make long casts and slowly swim the bait through them. I've had times when I'd make 50 casts to an area with a different bait, then switch to a plastic shad and catch eight or 10 fish in a row," he says.

Taylor finds summer and fall bass to be easier to catch on other lures, but the plastic shad option always lurks at the back of his mind. "When the fish are surfacing, you can catch them by swimming it through the school. And when they aren't on top, you can go to known schooling areas and fish a small bait on a spinning rig. I've caught several smallmouth on that pattern by hopping the bait on the rocks," he says.

In winter, the plastic shad again becomes a standard armament in Taylor's arsenal of lures. "The shad congregate in deep creeks, and when bass start feeding on them, they will push them into the shallow creeks and flats. Different species of fish will be mixed together, but you can catch a lot of big largemouth and smallmouth," he says.

waters connected to the Great Lakes.

Zona looks for eddies around current-breaking structure, such as barge pits and old, crumbling breakwalls. "The bass hold in the slack water," he explains. "When an alewife comes through, the smallmouth see a white flash and they eat it." He positions his boat on the downcurrent side of the structure and casts his lure across, bringing it along the same paths the baitfish follow.

During fall, when the wave of incoming alewives has passed, Zona turns his attention to flats ranging from 2 to 10 feet deep that lie within a few hundred yards of a timber-lined break into deeper water. He roams about, making random casts and quickly covering water with a fast, jerkbait-style retrieve as he looks for schools of marauding smallmouth.

He uses larger baits and heavier jigheads during the spawn, but at other times, Zona prefers 2-inch baits in pearl, smoke/silver flake or bluegill patterns. He rigs them on 1/8- to 3/8-ounce Hawg Hauler heads tied to spinning tackle via 6- to 8-pound-test Stren Super Tough line.

SASSY BASS

Call them whatever you want ...
they catch fish and lots of them

SHAD-BODIED grubs, typified by Mister Twister's Sassy Shad, are effective whenever bass are feeding on shad or herring. The key is to match the size of your lure to the size of the baitfish.

WHAT'S IN A NAME? Apparently, plenty. When Mister Twister introduced its soft plastic shad-bodied lures, Sassy Shads, in 1978, they quickly became a hot bait among striped bass anglers. These lively lures have a texture that closely matches that of a real shad, and when stripers grab one of these, they hold on.

Sassy Shads also are killer largemouth lures, but it's taken a new label — swimbaits — for an old lure to create another hot technique among bass anglers. For years, few bass anglers bothered with these lures, but they are quickly becoming a go-to pattern.

Although Sassy Shads were the original version of soft-bodied shad lures, a thousand other versions,

LITTLE LURES do indeed catch bass, especially in fall and spring, when bass are feeding aggressively in shallow water.

all essentially the same shape and texture, are on the market. They all work at one time or another and they won't cost you a $5 bill every time you lose one. Their unique, lifelike swimming action entices bass to bite when they might not otherwise hit a hard plastic bait.

SHAPING UP WITH SHAD

"I consider them my top secret weapon here on Lake Anna," says Chris McCotter, a guide on this 9,600-acre central Virginia reservoir. "They mimic so closely what the fish are feeding on."

The full-time guide admits that swimming these lures across flats and points isn't the most glamorous tactic, but it catches some tremendous bass when conditions are right. He likes to use them in the spring and fall, but says February and March are the prime months to throw them on his home lake. McCotter likes to heave his swimbaits as far as he can toward typical prespawn areas, such as points near the main creek channels and flats adjacent to deeper water.

"It's important to keep your rod tip up at about 11 o'clock as you reel this bait. That way you can feel strikes better. If you hold your rod tip too low, you'll miss a lot of bass. I'd say that's the No. 1 mistake my clients make when they use swimbaits. Also, the baits just run better when your rod tip is up," he says.

Like many reservoirs across the country, McCotter's home lake has both shad and herring, and he'll make every effort to match his baits not only to the size of the forage, but to the particular species. Some lures have a deeper belly than others, and shad and herring have a slightly differ-

ent profile, as well. McCotter will even throw a cast net to determine the type of bait in the area, or he may simply rely on an inspection of any baitfish a bass might have in its throat when he lands a fish.

SASSY PITCHING AND SKIPPING

Swimbaits, however, aren't just for swimming, says Texas guide and tournament angler Mark Hooker. Although he fishes them the same way most other anglers do, Hooker also works Sassy Shads like other anglers use jigs, finesse worms and tubes: He skips them far up under docks and overhanging limbs. Perhaps even more surprising than his technique is the way he rigs them.

"I'll use a 2/0 Mister Twister screw-lock keeper hook and a 3 1/2-inch Sassy Shad. I don't use any weight, but these lures are fairly heavy to begin with, so casting them isn't a problem. I just work the hook through the belly of the bait and bring it out the back, just like Texas rigging a lizard. It takes a little practice to get the bait rigged just right, but it's not that hard," he says. "They skip perfectly."

According to Hooker, this technique is excellent for those times when the bass just aren't interested in chasing a faster moving bait or something that drops quickly to the bottom and stays there. He'll use it just about anytime after the spawn is over and bass have moved to docks and other cover where they are tough to reach.

Soft Plastic Tip

A 2 1/2- or 3-inch shad tail grub is a superb alternative to topwater plugs when bass are in "the jumps" during late summer and fall. If schooling bass are only swiping at your topwaters, fire a little Sassy Shad into a swirl and let it fall briefly before swimming it back. The lures closely match the size of shad that school bass are after.

School Tactics

Mark Hooker breaks out the soft-bodied shad lures again in the summer and fall, when the bass on his home lakes school up and chase shad over open water. Like Monroe and McCotter, he sticks with smaller baits, usually a 3 1/2-inch Sassy Shad, and a light jighead.

"I almost never use a head heavier than 1/8 ounce because the bass are typically close to or right on the surface when I'm using these lures. You don't want it to sink too fast, but even with that lighter head, you can cast these things a mile," he says.

How he retrieves his lure depends entirely on the mood of the fish. Sometimes he'll score by burning it just under the surface; other times the bass want a slow, steady retrieve, or they may prefer to whack it as it slowly free-falls toward the bottom.

"You just have to try different things. I'll even use a yo-yo retrieve — letting it fall and then jerking it back up," he adds.

Hooker will use a 4-inch Sassy Shad if the fish are very active and he wants to target larger bass.

By skipping a flat-sided Sassy Shad, he can reach far up under cover, where few other lures can get. Of course, it takes a little practice to get the lure to do what you want it to, but like any technique that catches bass, this one is worth learning.

"It's a very subtle bait. I'll put it up under a dock and let it sink for a few seconds before I start to retrieve it. But I don't just start swimming it back to the boat. Instead, I'll twitch it as I retrieve it, just like I would a crippled shad," he notes.

BURNING RUBBER

California pro Ish Monroe also relies on shad-bodied baits for catching quality bass in the spring and fall. However, each season requires a different-size bait and a different application.

(Opposite page)
ISH MONROE uses rainbow trout
Optima Swim Baits during the
prespawn phase on lakes that are
stocked with the gamefish.

Color Matters

It may only be a matter of time before soft shadlike baits are available in dozens of different colors and combinations of colors, but right now, anglers have a fairly limited selection from which to choose. That's a good thing, agree Mark Hooker and Chris McCotter. Both guides follow the basic tenet that clear water dictates natural-looking baits, and dirty water calls for lures with at least some chartreuse on them. A dozen more color combinations might do little but confuse anglers.

"I'm a big fan of Mister Twister's bleeding shad Sassy Shad. I also really like the white pearl/black-back combination. That's about all I'll use in clear water," says Hooker.

McCotter sticks with pearl, salt-and-pepper and salt for clear water, and pepper with a chartreuse tail for dingy water.

"A killer spring pattern on Clear Lake — or any lake that is stocked with trout — is to burn a big rainbow trout Optima Swimbait off points and flats where prespawn bass will be," says Monroe. "It's a great prespawn pattern that takes some huge stringers of bass. I'd say that's my favorite time of year to throw these lures."

Optima's baits are pre-rigged with the body of the lure molded around the hook and the lead jighead. That means once the bait tears, you have to get a new one. You can't simply replace the body like you can with other soft shad-bodied lures. Although that may seem like a costly way to catch bass, Monroe figures he gets about 20 fish on each lure before he has to get a new one. That's a fair trade. If you want to use a cheaper version, try a 6- or 8-inch Sassy Shad or a generic shad body — marketed primarily to saltwater striped bass anglers — rigged on a 1/2- to 1-ounce jighead.

The Top 150 angler uses a standard chuck-and-wind retrieve, adding that the purpose of these baits is to imitate a disoriented rainbow trout, as if it were just stocked and still confused about its new surroundings. In other words, it imitates an easy, nutritious meal. Sometimes Monroe burns them just under the surface; other times he uses a slow, steady retrieve.

These are big baits, however, so it's important to use heavy tackle to send them to the right places. Monroe relies on an 8-foot Lamiglas rod that was designed specifically for these large swimbaits. He'll use lures up to 8 inches long and 3 ounces, tied to 25-pound Excalibur Silver Thread monofilament. Although such a heavy line can stand out like day-glo anchor rope in air clear water, Monroe doesn't worry about that, insisting this pattern elicits a reaction bite.

"Never make a standard overhead cast. You need to make a sidearm cast, and you need to lob these lures instead of using a standard fast cast. You'll break your rod if you do that," he explains.

MATCH THE HATCH

In the fall, McCotter and Monroe like to throw smaller shad-bodied baits in the backs of creeks. They believe 2 1/2-inch Sassy Shads match the young-of-the-year shad quite well, and actively feeding bass will gorge on these smaller baitfish as the water cools. Monroe will even drop down to a 1-inch shad rigged on a 1/8-ounce head for those days when bass are extra-tough to catch.

"I'll target channels toward the backs of creeks. I'll either look for shad flipping on the surface or, ideally, bass busting bait on the surface. It's real important to match the size of your lure to the size of the bait," he says.

Specifically, Monroe targets those high percentage areas in the backs of creeks — bends in the channel, points that extend into the creek channel and stumps, rocks and brush adjacent to dropoffs.

McCotter likes a 7-foot Berkley Lightning Rod and a G-4 Ultracast reel loaded with 12-pound Berkley Sensation line. He'll drop down to 10-pound line in clearer water, but he isn't worried about losing fish in heavy cover, since he typically throws these lures in open water.

WHEN ADDING weight to a soft jerkbait, be careful not to add too much, unless you intend to fish the bait on the bottom. Too much weight negates the darting, dipping characteristic of the lure.

EXPANDED ROLES FOR SOFT JERKBAITS

These buoyant plastic lures are deadly near the surface and not half-bad on the bottom, either

FEW SOFT PLASTIC LURES have impacted the sport of bass fishing recently with the force of Lunker City Specialties' Slug-Go.

A simplistic piece of plastic with an irresistible, built-in erratic action, the Slug-Go created a new category of lures, the soft jerkbaits. It accounted for tournament victories and impressive catches wherever it went in the early 1990s.

Back then, Connecticut angler Herb Reed's invention quickly earned a place in the tackleboxes of bass enthusiasts everywhere.

A major reason for the immediate, newfound fondness for the Slug-Go — apart from its ability to attract strikes — is the easy, "no-brainer" effort it takes to work the bulky plastic creature effectively. Most fishermen simply twitch and pause the lure on or near the surface, and that rhythmic movement is often enough to draw attention from below.

(Opposite page) A SCREW-IN worm sinker works best when weighting a soft jerkbait because it blends in with the lure's action instead of working against it.

But the angler who limits himself to the traditional method of working a soft jerkbait is undoubtedly missing out on the real fun of fishing these lures — and he fails to take full advantage of their allure. Soft jerkbaits are extremely versatile tools in the hands of adventurous fishermen.

"The Slug-Go is a lot more of a lure than just a visual topwater lure," Reed emphasizes. "But 90 percent of the people throw it out, twitch-twitch-twitch it, bring it in and that's it. Even if nothing bites it, that's the only way they fish it.

"I think everybody — especially tournament fishermen — is conditioned to fishing so fast that they leave a lot of fish behind, because they're looking for something that wants to bite a quick bait.

Soft Plastic Tip

A strike, whether or not it results in a hookup, can reveal important facts about the mood of the bass, but you have to pay attention. By noting where the lure landed and where the bass intercepted it, you can determine how actively the fish are feeding, where they are positioned and how best to retrieve the lure.

USE A soft jerkbait as a follow-up tactic to fish that strike and miss a reaction bait like a spinnerbait.

They get into a Rat-L-Trap or spinnerbait rhythm and never really slow down enough to fish thoroughly. The more you can slow down, the more bites you will get in an area, even with a Slug-Go."

WORMING A SLUG-GO

Some anglers have discovered that soft jerkbaits can be absolutely deadly when rigged and fished methodically like a conventional plastic worm — particularly in submerged vegetation and standing timber. And some of their results have been spectacular.

"That approach to fishing the Slug-Go doesn't surprise me, particularly when you have weeds," Reed interjects. "The advantage a Slug-Go has over a swimming-style worm is that the bait won't grab onto weeds or other cover. I know of some guys who have won tournaments by flipping them down into potholes in the weeds for that exact reason — it just drops in and slides right through the cover.

"If you've ever tried dropping a worm through hyacinths or any thick vegetation, you know that the tail is always catching on the weeds, whereas the Slug-Go just plummets right through the stuff."

A prime example of this worming strategy was the winning method used by the amateur champion of a BASS tournament held on Georgia's Lake Seminole. What is most impressive is Perry Burke, the winner, used the technique from the back of the boat to weigh in nearly 40 pounds of bass.

"I was trying to do something different from the pro to catch fish, because the pro has control of the boat and first shot at every good spot," Burke says. "And this was a technique I had used quite a bit. In fact, I caught eight bass weighing 62 pounds on Seminole in the fall using this technique.

"This technique isn't well known because jerkbaits are something that everybody twitches on top around standing timber and deep grass in this lake," Burke recalled. "But I sometimes work it like a worm. I don't twitch it. Every time I pick it up, I just shake it like I'm trying to get grass off, then I drop it back down to the bottom."

INSERTING A roofing nail into the middle of a soft jerkbait makes it fall horizontally.

Stevens had discovered that the Lake Seminole bass were bedding in flooded timber in about 8 feet of water. The fish were either at the base of the tree or any flat crook in its trunk, about 4 feet under the surface. For this situation, Stevens inserted a small nail-like weight developed by Lunker City into a 6-inch Slug-Go, which made the lure stand straight as it rested on the bottom. The weight was positioned in the middle of the jerkbait (just behind a 5/0 wide gap hook) along with a rattle chamber.

"I worked it exactly like a worm," he remembers. "I just let it fall and then pulled it up. I would pull it up to the crotch of the tree and then jiggle it. And I would let it sit on the bed. The bass usually hit it as it dropped straight down along the tree."

This offbeat Slug-Go technique has scored for Stevens in the past on prespawn and spawning bass in the stumpfields of Florida's Rodman Reservoir. It has also worked for him throughout the

THE ADVANTAGE a soft jerkbait has over a floating worm is the former bait will not grab onto weeds or other cover.

spring along weed edges and interior pockets in several northern lakes. And it has proved productive around concrete seawalls, as well.

Stevens was asked to theorize why this method works.

"When you pull it off a weed and then feed it line like crazy, it goes straight down and stands up on the bottom," he says. "It doesn't have a curled tail like a plastic worm, so I think it resembles a freshwater eel, which is a common sight to bass, particularly in Florida.

"Plus, it's something different that the fish haven't seen before."

BOTTOM BUMPING

The value of bottom bumping a soft jerkbait isn't lost on soft plastic sage Larry Nixon.

"Some of the biggest fish I've ever caught on a Slug-Go or Riverside Big Gun came in 6 to 10 feet of water, when I just let it sink to the bottom," he says. "Occasionally, you'll see a big fish come up on a bait like a spinnerbait and not take it — then you know where it lives.

"In that situation, I'll sneak back later and throw a soft jerkbait that's weighted and just kill it over the spot. I feed it slack so it sinks right into the ambush point. It's a great trick for times when bass aren't active and you know where they are positioned."

BASS tournament king Roland Martin takes that particular technique south of the border to Mexico's Lake Baccarac and enjoys some remarkable success.

Martin's best trophy action comes by working a huge, 9-inch Slug-Go around submerged trees in 5 to 10 feet of water.

"I only fish that big Slug-Go in the mornings, and I can usually catch five or six bass over 6 pounds," he says. "That's on the small side of the scale. I've caught them up to 9 and 12 pounds.

"I rig this big, humongous Slug-Go with a huge 8/0 hook and a little 1/8-ounce Florida rig screw-in sinker so that it will sink a little bit. You throw it in the trees and let it sink down like a worm. Most of the big fish hit it as it sinks. I let it sink and dead-line it; many times the fish will be on it when I pick it up the first time."

Soft jerkbaits can be utilized to quickly cover acres and acres of water in search of active bass. And that is probably their greatest asset. But there are times that a soft jerkbait is most effective when its role is reversed and it takes on a slower, bottom-hugging appearance.

Jerkbait Tricks

Slug-Go inventor Herb Reed shares a few tricks and tips for his and other manufacturers' soft jerkbaits:

■ Using an offset hook, he rigs it in different places to change the action of the lure. For example, in shallow water where he wants to create a disturbance on the surface, Reed positions the hook farther back in the body of the Slug-Go to make it jump and pop out of the water like a frantic baitfish.

■ Give some consideration to how you weight a Slug-Go, he says. If you weight the bait too much, you're going to get the same action over and over — which is exactly the opposite reason why the Slug-Go is so effective. The secret is its erratic action. He usually inserts weight in the belly near the hook, which makes it more keel-weighted and gives it a better action as it drops through the water.

■ Two tricks for short-striking bass: First, switch colors. If that doesn't solve the problem, add a treble hook as a "stinger" to the main hook (inserting one of the three treble points into the plastic).

■ Insert weight in the nose of the lure and rig an exposed hook near the tail. This causes the bait to wiggle and swim. With a weighted nose, it stands up on the bottom when fished slowly.

■ For heavy vegetation and thick lily pads, Reed adds a weedguard made from a strong piece of monofilament or toothpick to protect the slightly exposed hook. "Stick the heavy mono or toothpick in the back of the Slug-Go and snip it right in front of the hook," he says. "It will act like a weedguard so you can get it through the pads. Yet, when the fish bite down on it, even the toothpick is flexible enough to just move right down out of the way."

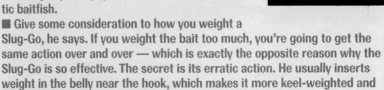

KELLY JORDON says that combining a pair of Lake Fork MegaWeight tungsten sinkers creates more noise and attracts more bites.

the bottom, and because of the limited stretch, you can set the hook on a fish at the end of a cast and in deep water. If you do snag, the monofilament will break, so all you need to replace is the leader."

Yelas agrees, saying that braid is a good choice for rigging in heavy winds because the smaller diameter creates less drag.

"You don't get as much bow in the line as you do with thicker line, so you detect strikes better," he explains.

Yelas also recommends fluorocarbon as a leader material, particularly in clear water. Fluorocarbon is more sensitive, durable and less visible than monofilament. However, fluorocarbon sinks faster, so it may not be the best choice if you want your bait to hover off the bottom.

When fishing around heavier cover in deep water, Bird uses 30-pound monofilament as his leader.

"The thicker line doesn't sink as fast, and it will help keep your bait off the bottom," he notes.

Sinker size can affect line choice, too. Most pros prefer a weight that gets to the bottom quickly and enables them to feel the structure or bottom content. However, when fishing shallower water or with lighter line in ultraclear water, a lighter sinker may do the job.

A smaller sinker is best for fishing grass because it is less likely to clog in the vegetation. You can lessen the drag through grass by choosing a more streamlined bullet- or cylindrical Mojo-style weight.

"I'll also switch to a straight shank hook rather than an offset design," adds Rook. "The bend in the offset is great for keeping soft plastics from sliding down the hook shank, but it really catches in the grass."

Several anglers now use sinkers made of tungsten material because they are extremely hard; hence, they transmit more bottom sensations and are 25 percent smaller than lead sinkers.

CAROLINA PLASTICS

Anglers who are open-minded about lure choices catch more fish, says Rook. While lizards, French fries and worms are mainstays, less notable lures can be deadly.

"A lot of fishermen fish the traditional baits, and when they aren't working, they give up," he explains. "I've found that trying different colors, sizes or styles of lures can make a difference."

Thliveros agrees. Two of his favorite Carolina rig lures are the Zoom Fluke and flipping-size tube baits. Both are effective in the fall, when bass are targeting baitfish.

The sage pro drags both lures the same way he does traditional Carolina rig baits, but notes that the actions may be different enough to catch the bass' eyes.

WINDY WEATHER can dictate line choice. Jay Yelas suggests using braided line to offset heavy winds.

THE PRIMARY advantage of a drop shot rig is that it holds the bait up where bass easily see it when the weight touches the bottom.

DEEPER INTO DROP SHOTTING

There's more than one way to catch a bass on this Western finesse rig. Try these tips the next time you encounter a tough bite on your home waters

GIVEN THE SUCCESS Californian Aaron Martens has enjoyed fishing bass tournaments across the country, it's obvious he's learned how to adapt to different types of waters.

Even so, his favorite technique remains drop shotting, the light line spinning presentation that scores big on ultraclear Western impoundments. Though many anglers believe drop shotting has limited applications east of the Continental Divide, Martens believes otherwise.

(Opposite page) MARK KILE fishes a drop shot worm above a standard Texas rigged finesse worm. The bullet weight for the latter serves as the drop shot weight.

He's already proved the point by nearly winning tournaments east of the Mississippi River, including a near miss on South Carolina's Lake Murray.

Martens didn't catch all his fish at Murray by drop shotting, but the method did account for bass he wouldn't have netted otherwise. He was fishing a worm around deep docks and planted brushpiles about 20 feet deep.

"I caught most of my fish at Murray on a Texas rig," says Martens. "During midday, the bite got tough, and a drop shot rig worked really well. I was casting mainly to brushpiles, and working the drop shot right down into the limbs. Whenever the bite is tough and nothing's working, I'll try drop shotting. It's my go-to rig."

Fishing a drop shot in cover is at odds with the deep, vertical presentation for which this method is known. When he won a BASS tournament at Lake Oroville, Calif., Martens plucked spotted bass from rocky ledges as deep as 130 feet with a 1/4-ounce weight, 6-pound line, a 3-foot leader and a Robo

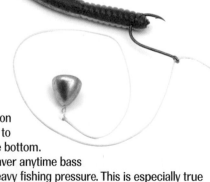

Soft Plastic Tip

Drop shot rigs work throughout the year and are especially productive in the fall. Autumn is when bass key on baitfish and are more inclined to nab lures presented above the bottom. But a drop shot can be a lifesaver anytime bass have grown lure-shy due to heavy fishing pressure. This is especially true for anglers who are willing to take drop shot fishing in new directions.

Body Shad impaled with a tiny exposed hook. He claims it took the rig two minutes to sink to the bottom. At Murray, Martens coaxed largemouths from brushpiles with a 1/4-ounce weight, 10-pound-test line, a 12-inch leader, and a 2/0 straight shank Gamakatsu worm hook rigged Texas style on a Robo Zipper Shaker Worm.

Martens' drop shot variations don't end there. During the Bassmaster Classic in Chicago, he made impressive catches of smallmouth bass by swimming a 1/16-ounce drop shot rig with a Robo Body Shad tight to riprap in 1 to 3 feet of water. He claims he outfished competitors in the same area 4-to-1. He has also pulled largemouth from shallow cover while pitching a 3/8- to 1/2-ounce drop shot rig with a stiff baitcasting outfit, 15-pound line and a bulky bait, such as a Zoom Brush Hog rigged Texas style.

"People just don't realize all the things they can do with a drop shot rig," says Martens. "Sometimes I'll cast it and hop it over the bottom quickly, like you would a jig. If I'm fishing grass growing on the bottom, I'll go to a 24-inch-or-longer leader to keep the bait above it. You can bait the hook with a (Zoom) Fluke, a trick worm, anything you want."

The primary advantage of the drop shot rig is that it holds the bait up where bass easily see it when the weight touches bottom. By adjusting the length of the drop line, you keep the bait working precisely in a given strike zone.

Twitching the line with the rod tip brings the bait to life in a manner that can't be duplicated with any other technique. When fishing vertically, the bait dances seductively in one place as long as necessary to goad reluctant bass into striking. Hop or drag the weight, and the bait swims along with the action of a live minnow. Pause the retrieve and give a little slack line, and the bait drifts slowly, irresistibly, toward bottom.

The drop shot also sinks fast, which is a decided advantage in deep water. Since the weight is separated from the bait, it transmits stronger signals up the line and helps the angler detect cover and changes in bottom composition.

While the basic drop shot rig is essentially the same as when Martens began experimenting with it four years ago, recent tackle improvements have made it more efficient. The most significant advancements have been with the weight.

Lead bell sinkers and large split shot sufficed initially. Then came round lead weights molded around a swivel that sprouts an elongated, quick-change line eye. Tie a knot in the end of the line, run it through the eye and pull the line up into the narrow slot. The quick-change device grabs the line so tightly, many anglers don't bother with a knot.

The quick-change line eye lets you switch

Palomar Knot Trick

When drop shot fishing, the hook should ride up to ensure better action and a higher hooking percentage. An easy way to accomplish the correct hook posture is to tie a Palomar knot with a tag line long enough to serve as the drop line to the weight. Then hold the hook with the point up and run the tag line through the hook's eye, from top to bottom. Attach a drop weight to the tag line, and you're good to go.

TO TIE A DROP SHOT RIG, double the line and pass it through the hook eye. Tie an overhand knot in the doubled line and slip the loop over the hook. Tighten, then run the tag end through the hook eye, from top to bottom.

weights in seconds. Should the weight snag, the quick-change eye cuts the line before the whole rig breaks off. Then you can quickly attach another drop weight and continue fishing.

Cylinder-shaped finesse weights were next in the drop shot evolution, and they are available with standard swivels and quick-change line eyes. These slender weights excel when you're fishing snag-infested bottoms that eat round shot like candy.

Fluorocarbon line has also been a boon to drop shotters, especially when bass are deep.

"Fluorocarbon line sinks faster than monofilament," says New Jersey's Kotaro Kiriyama, who claims he fishes a drop shot rig more than 50 percent of the time. "And because it has less stretch, Fluorocarbon gives me better feel. I don't miss as many fish with it.

"I like to drag a drop shot rig because I can feel any cover or little drops or dips in the bottom," says Kiriyama. "If you hop the weight, you miss those subtle differences. Whenever I feel something good, like rocks, I stop dragging and twitch the line. I catch a lot of bass doing that."

With light line spinning applications, Kiriyama wields a 6 1/2-foot Shimano graphite rod in a medium action. Some accomplished drop shotters, including Martens, prefer a medium light spinning rod, due to the light line and the tiny, open hooks that are often employed. But Kiriyama believes a light action rod is forgiving enough and provides better feel, surer hook sets and more control over the lure.

"When you fish a wimpy rod in deep water, it's hard to jiggle the bait because the long line has a dampening effect," says Kiriyama. "With a stiffer rod, I can put action into the bait without making unusually big rod movements."

A medium light spinning rod is the choice of Arizona angler Mark Kile when he fishes a drop shot in deep water, a method that has helped him garner high finishes in western BASS tournaments. When he makes a vertical presentation to deep bass, Kile merely opens the bail on his spinning rod and lets the drop shot plummet to the bottom.

"You can't beat a spinning outfit for fishing vertically," says Kile. "A lot of times I'll move around slowly with the electric motor and look for bass with my Lowrance X-15 graph. When I mark a fish, I immediately drop the bait straight down to it. I have a lot of success with that approach."

Another ploy that puts bass in Kile's livewell is a double rig. One basic setup consists of a standard Texas rigged worm with a tiny drop shot bait 12 to 18 inches above the worm. The bullet sinker on the Texas rig serves as the drop shot weight, while the extra bait hovering above the worm shows bass an entirely different look.

"A double rig covers two depths at the same time," says Kile. "If you get into a school of bass, it's not unusual to catch two at a time. When you hook a bass, other bass are drawn to the struggle, and one of them often pounces on the second bait."

A drop shot bait above a spider jig or tube jig also yields bass for Kile. He sometimes rigs a drop shot bait above the sinker on a Carolina rig. Kile opts for the Carolina combo when he needs to cover a lot of water.

MARK KILE says drop shotting pays dividends whenever bass are hit with heavy fishing pressure. Here, he fishes for shallow bass relating to a launch ramp, a spot that often produces bass released after previous tournaments.

WHEN DRIFTING a finesse worm to a fallen tree, use the current to deliver the lure to the fish.

STREAMING SOFT PLASTICS
If you're serious about stream fishing, learn all you can about fishing soft plastics in moving water

MOST BASS FISHERMEN VIEW stream fishing as a pleasant, if infrequent, diversion from big water angling. Not George Verrusio. This Coatesville, Ind., stream guru is as serious about creek fishing as any tournament angler is about reservoir or lake fishing.

He's caught many lunker bass from streams, including smallmouth over 5 pounds, and he approaches these small waters with the same level of analytical skill that bass pros employ on their tournament venues.

Here, Verrusio reveals inside tips on fishing soft baits you can use to tap into the biggest fish in your area streams.

(Opposite page) WHETHER YOU wade or float a bass stream, soft plastics are perfect for getting inactive and well-hidden bass to strike.

SEVENTY PERCENT SOLUTION

"Around 70 percent of the time, a soft plastic lure will be your best choice for stream bass," Verrusio says. "There are situations where other lures, including buzzbaits, topwater plugs or crankbaits, may outproduce them, but for consistency and quality fish, you can't beat soft plastics."

Verrusio didn't always feel that way. "Like most stream fishermen, I started out using in-line spinners and small plugs extensively. While these will definitely catch creek bass, I found I was fishing them too fast to connect with the big fish I was after. Also, the more time I spent in the water, the more I learned about the kinds of places where stream bass live. You can't fish treble-hooked lures in these spots."

Soft plastics offer many advantages to the stream angler, Verrusio points out. "They're highly portable, which I view as a real positive when I'm wading. You don't really need a tacklebox — just stuff a selection of soft baits, leadheads and hooks in plastic bags and cram 'em in your pockets; (but don't try this with treble-hook lures).

"You can fish them tight to cover where big

Soft Plastic Tip

Fish a soft jerkbait when bass are in slack water on the edge of a gravel flat with scattered grass patches. Just don't overdo it. Stream bass are turned off by an overactive presentation in clear, slack water. Just twitch the bait gently as it suspends around the grass.

stream bass lurk. They're inexpensive, too. If you get hung up and don't want to wade through a good hole to untangle the lure, just break off and retrieve it later. With their infinite variety of sizes, shapes and colors, they make it easy to match the hatch. And most important, they're the most natural of all stream lures, even when fished superslow in clear water."

GEORGE'S MENU

Among the soft plastics Verrusio highly recommends for stream use are the following:

Leadhead grubs — "If you use only one type of soft plastic, make it a grub. These are the deadliest of all stream lures, especially in clear water, where they resemble minnows. I use 3- and 4-inch curled-tails. Grubs work everywhere from shallow shoals to deep holes. The only wrong way to fish them is to not use them."

Finesse worms — "I've experimented extensively with short, skinny worms such as Charlie Brewer's Slider and Kalin's Weenie Worm. They're deadly in cold water when bass won't respond to a more active lure, and are my top choice for stream bass buried in dense cover."

Leeches — "Live leeches are important creek bass forage, and a soft plastic leech will draw vicious strikes, especially from smallmouth. I like to swim these slowly near the bottom in fast current to get that rippling action out of the tail."

Soft craws — "Crawfish are among the most prevalent forage species in rocky streams. Fish a soft craw on the bottom, retrieving with occa-

sional short jerks of the rod tip. Excellent around ledge rock and sunken logs."

Soft jerkbaits — "I've only recently begun using these in streams, and have been encouraged by the results. They're exciting to fish; usually you can see the bass swim up and take the lure. Try both 4- and 6-inch versions rigged weightless on a light wire worm hook, keeping the hook point just barely buried back into the lure body. Fish them close to wood and grass cover."

Tube baits — "Killer creek lures! The clearer and more highly pressured the stream, the better you'll do on them. Insert some foam in a tube and it'll float — a deadly presentation when there's an insect hatch on the water."

Hellgrammite imitators — "Hellgrammites are like candy to stream smallies, so fish these baits tight to bottom, around gravel and chunk rock."

WHERE TO STREAM

Soft plastics don't work everywhere, our expert claims, but insists they outshine all other lures in a wide variety of stream situations. "They are especially productive in clear streams, because of their realistic appearance and movements. Unlike spinners and crankbaits, which have built-in action, the movements of a soft plastic lure can be controlled almost totally by the angler. By twitching or shaking the rod tip, you can give the lure as much or as little action as you deem necessary to provoke a bass into striking."

Verrusio also likes soft plastics in stained water.

THE LEADHEAD jig and grub is the most basic combination for stream fishing.

"If there's at least a foot of visibility, I'll use soft baits, but their productivity falls off once the water begins to get muddy. Incidentally, I've had better luck on soft plastics in a clearing stream than in one that's turning murky, but don't ask me why."

The colder the water, the more you should reach for soft baits, he notes. "Most hard baits have way too much action for sluggish bass in cold streams. Soft plastics can be fished extremely slow and still draw strikes."

Likewise, these lures outperform all others on highly pressured creeks. "If I see signs that other anglers have been down to the stream recently, like fresh tire tracks near the access point, I'll always use soft baits and a slow, methodical approach," he adds.

Fish soft plastics as tight to cover as possible: "When bass are actively feeding, which is about 15 percent of the time, you'll get strikes right out in open water," Verrusio declares. "I've seen smallmouth rush to grab a swimming grub from 30 feet away in clear streams. But you're far more likely to find stream bass wary and holding tight to cover, which calls for a saturation approach."

Verrusio points out that there are three basic types of presentations you can make in a stream: (1) from a downstream position, (2) from an upstream position and (3) across the current.

STREAM SCENARIOS

The following likely scenarios were proposed to Verrusio. What follows are his recommendations for each situation.

● Bass are holding in midstream logjams.

"First try to pull the fish out of the slop with an active lure like a grub. But if they don't show themselves, march right up to the cover and 'doodle' a finesse worm rigged weedless. Simply lower the worm into holes in the tangles and shake the rod tip gently so the lure dances in place on the bottom. I've caught some of my biggest stream bass doing this."

● Bass are beneath floating debris in an eddy pocket.

"Two things to remember about eddies: They're baitfish magnets, and when bass are in them, they're geared up to feed aggressively. Allowing a soft jerkbait to settle slowly around the spinning surface debris will often draw a quick strike. Or try darting a grub with a light-reflecting flake finish around the debris, rigging it with a 1/16-ounce head to keep it off the bottom."

● Bass are in a deep gravel-bottom hole.

"The biggest fish will stay tight to bottom, so imitate bottom-oriented forage with a finesse worm, hellgrammite or soft craw. Use enough weight to keep the lure down, and fish it with a slow, erratic retrieve. Deep water has less visibility, so help the bass find your lure by bulking up its size a bit and trying dark colors."

● Bass are in slack water on the edge of a gravel flat with scattered grass patches.

"A perfect spot for a soft jerkbait, but don't overfish it — stream bass are easily turned off by an overactive presentation in clear, slack water. Just twitch it gently as it suspends around the grass. If you see a big fish come out and grab it, don't panic — drop the rod tip, count to three and set the hook."

More Tips For Soft Plastic Streaming

Stream expert George Verrusio offers these additional tips for better creek bassin' with soft plastics:

■ Use light wire hooks with these lures. If you get hung up, tightening down hard will often straighten the hook so you can retrieve your lure without wading through productive water and spooking bass.

■ Leave vibrant-hued soft baits out in the sun for a few days before fishing them in ultraclear streams. They'll fade to a more realistic, drab color.

■ An ultralight rod is not a good choice for soft plastic lures. It lacks hook setting power and the backbone needed to handle the occasional big fish you'll encounter when using them. Verrusio uses a 6 1/2-foot Shimano spinning rod with a fast tip. A long rod like this permits long casts and helps keep your line off the water in current. Use abrasion-resistant 6- or 8-pound line and retie often.

■ Let the current work for you. In hard-to-reach places, such as a root tangle, try free-lining a soft bait so it floats into the target area.

■ If bass follow your soft lure but aren't striking, try pinching it off a little to shorten it, or change color to a more natural shade.

■ Remember that soft plastics aren't "bird-dog" lures like crankbaits and spinnerbaits. Instead of trying to cover a lot of water with them, remember that 90 percent of the bass in the stream will be in 10 percent of the water. Use soft plastics to probe that 10 percent thoroughly.

FLOATING WORMS draw strikes around shallow brush, logs, docks and other areas used by postspawn fish using the cover on their migrations back to deeper water.

POSTSPAWN PLASTICS

Fishing plans can unravel quickly in the transition period between the spawn and summer

POLL THE PROS AND MORE THAN LIKELY the postspawn will be the unanimous choice as the toughest of all the bass fishing cycles. The frustrating part of this angling conundrum is it follows the beginning of the fishing season for many anglers — the spawn — when big females are seen cruising the shallows.

Read on for advice from postspawn experts willing to offer their wisdom, or in some cases, condolences, to those of you who are oftentimes victimized by this sometimes frustrating time.

(Opposite page) ONE OF Jay Yelas' most productive postspawn tactics is to fish a floating worm around grass-beds and sparse brush near secondary tributary points.

BACON BITS

Veteran Missouri BASS pro Basil Bacon has competed in thousands of tournaments in a career that began in the 1960s, when the sport of competitive bass fishing first took flight. He's caught bass during postspawn in almost every state in the nation as well as several foreign countries, providing him rare insight into the behavior of our favorite fish during this often frustrating season.

"All bass don't spawn at once," Bacon emphasizes. "If they did, a major cold front or sudden drop in the lake's level could totally trash the spawn, eliminating an entire year-class of bass from the lake. Instead, spawning occurs in waves. Some fish go on the bed early, then as they leave, others move into the shallows to nest, and so on. This is nature's way of helping assure a successful spawn. In most lakes, an increasing number of bass will be in a postspawn mode when the water temperature climbs into the 70s, but even then, there will be a few fish left on the bed."

In clear, rocky lakes where shallow cover may be scarce, bass transition to deep points after spawning, calling for a totally different approach. Bacon often finds them suspending off these points anywhere

Soft Plastic Tip

What's the surest way to tell when bass have finished spawning? Check the surface temperature when you first launch your boat in the morning, not later in the day after the sun has warmed the water. The morning temperature will be a truer indication of whether bass will be on or off the bed.

UPGRADING TO larger tubes also increases the odds of landing bigger bronzebacks.

CAROLINA RIGS FOR SMALLIES

These innovative lures and techniques are proving adept at catching the biggest bronzebacks around

THINK WHAT YOU'D LEARN about bass if you went down among them four or five times a day. Greg Horoky ponders that notion every time he takes clients smallmouth fishing in western Lake Erie, from Colchester, Ontario. This small Canadian port, from which Horoky conducts a guide business, also accommodates Shipwreck Tours, an operation that provides a window to the underwater world. Mike Mullen, owner and operator of this unique enterprise, carries groups of passengers out several times a day in a small ferryboat he has converted to a tourist attraction.

(Opposite page) GREG HOROKY believes big smallmouth prefer substantial baits, and when feeding, they suspend above smaller bass.

After anchoring near one of 16 shipwrecks strewn over Erie's bottom within a short distance of Colchester, Mullen dons scuba gear and plunges into the water with a video camera connected to a cable. As he swims about the wreck, the images captured by the camera appear "live" on television monitors inside the boat.

Since the rocky bottom structures around Colchester comprise ideal smallmouth habitat, Mullen and his customers have seen countless bass while viewing the mysterious hulks of dead ships. Every time he goes fishing, Horoky asks Mullen the same question: "Where are the big smallmouth today?"

Mullen's reply never varies: "Where they always are, 4 feet above the bottom."

"It doesn't matter," says Horoky, "whether there's a cold front, a warm front, or whether it's windy, calm or muggy, full moon, no moon — the biggest bass always suspend 4 feet off bottom, often over the highest spot on a piece of structure."

Horoky's fishing experiences support the diver's observations. Many of the bigger smallmouth Horoky catches engulf tubes or curled-tail grubs before the lures ever reach bottom. This leads him to believe that smallmouth bass have a pecking order and that the

Soft Plastic Tip

As the prespawn season progresses, bass will move to the inside edge of a breakline, especially if cover is present, before heading onto the spawning flat. But don't concentrate all your efforts in one spot. The fish don't all spawn together, so be conscious that even though fish have left the breakline, others are likely moving up behind them to take their place.

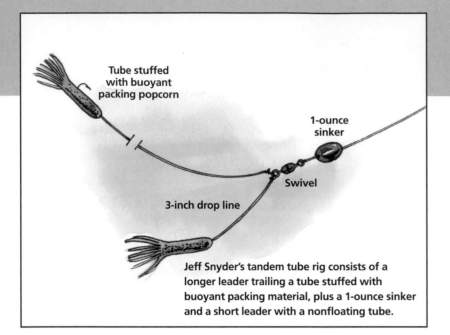

Tube stuffed with buoyant packing popcorn

1-ounce sinker

Swivel

3-inch drop line

Jeff Snyder's tandem tube rig consists of a longer leader trailing a tube stuffed with buoyant packing material, plus a 1-ounce sinker and a short leader with a nonfloating tube.

bigger fish station themselves above subordinates, where they can get first crack at any baitfish cruising past.

Another theory came to Horoky while fishing emerald shiners with clients who prefer to use live bait. Most of the shiners he purchases run 3 1/2 to 4 inches in length. If smallmouth are in the area, it usually doesn't them take long to warm up to the shiners.

"Once in a while," says Horoky, "we'll inadvertently get a 6-inch shad or shiner in with the regular minnows. Whenever we drop down one of those big baits, a smallmouth jumps on it immediately. And that's usually a good fish."

TUBING

Horoky is a big fan of plastic tubes, and he thinks big, opting for the 4- to 6-inch sizes.

"We Carolina rig them," says Horoky. "Bass really love their bulky profile. When we want to catch numbers of average bass, we go with a short leader, say, 2 feet, to keep the bait near bottom. If we go to a 3- to 6-foot leader, the tube floats higher and catches the bigger, dominant fish."

The first time Horoky tried Carolina rigging with a tube, he fished a local buddy tournament out of Colchester on a day when the smallmouth were slow to bite. He and his partner fished rocky offshore humps alongside other competitors and culled a winning limit from nearly 30 bass. Most other anglers struggled to boat five 12-inch fish.

"We can now catch suspended bass, which have been so elusive in the past," says Horoky.

When weighted with a 3/4-ounce sinker, a Carolina rigged tube swims high over Lake Erie's rock/rubble bottom structures. Horoky rigs it with a straight-shank 3/0 or 4/0 hook, tip exposed, and he rarely snags. He runs the hook's shank between the inside wall of the tube and the foam insert, and out the nose of the bait.

Given the predominantly windy conditions that occur on Lake Erie, Horoky and fishing partner Bill Gitlin usually drift and drag the Carolina rigged tube. Should the breeze push the boat too fast for the weight to maintain consistent bottom contact, they set out a windsock to slow the drift.

"Just drag the bait," says Gitlin. "The less you do with it, the better. The bass are used to seeing things float by at the same speed the current is moving. Whenever the sinker hits and bounces off rocks, the tube starts and stops and hangs in a bass' face. They pounce on it like a cat."

When casting or fishing from an anchored position, Gitlin slides the sinker ahead to increase bottom contact and impart more action to the tube. He suggests using Fireline, Fusion or another of the superlines for the leader material.

"Because these lines float and have virtually no stretch," says Gitlin, "they enhance the erratic action of the tube."

TANDEM TUBES

Ohioan Jeff Snyder, a veteran of many BASS tournaments, often catches Great Lakes smallmouth above bottom with tubes, but he does so with different approaches than those used by Horoky and Gitlin. One is the tandem tube Carolina Rig. This combination consists of a Carolina rigged tube stuffed with packing popcorn (not the type that dissolves in water) so it floats above bottom. Snyder rigs the tube with a bare, unweighted jig hook and leaves the point exposed.

A second tube is connected to the lower end of the swivel with a 3-inch drop line. As the 1-ounce sinker scrapes rocks and boulders, it attracts bottom-feeding bass to the dropper tube. Meanwhile, bass cruising above bottom zero-in on the tube floating 3 to 4 feet behind the weight.

Though not a Carolina rig, another tandem setup that works well for Snyder starts with a 1/4- or 3/8-ounce tube jig tied to a rod spooled with 8-pound-test monofilament. Snyder cuts the line above the tube at whatever depth he feels the smallmouth are holding over bottom, typically 3 to 5 feet. He ties the line from the tube to a swivel. The line from the rod is threaded through one end of another swivel and tied to the swivel connected to the tube.

A second tube is rigged with a plain jig hook and attached to the free-sliding swivel with a 12-inch drop line. As the weighted tube plays tag with the bottom, the tube on the drop line swims merrily along, where it is more easily spotted by smallmouth suspended above bottom. Snyder usually drifts and drags his tandem tube rigs, but they also may be cast and retrieved.

"I can't say that I catch bigger smallmouth on the higher tubes," says Snyder. "What these tandem rigs do is let me cover two different zones at once. I get a lot of action with them. Doubles are common."

Snyder finds that scraping bottom with tubes fares better in spring and fall, when smallmouth key on crawfish — and anytime baitfish hug bottom. In summer, when baitfish spend more time up off the bottom, tubes running higher get more attention.

CAROLINA LIZARDS

The standard Carolina rig also is proving its effectiveness on smallmouth bass in the Great Lakes, smaller natural lakes and impoundments.

Most anglers opt for 3- to 4-inch baits when targeting smallmouth. They like smaller tubes, reapers, French fry worms and miniature lizards. Kentuckian Scott Patton also catches smallmouth by Carolina rigging diminutive baits, but he generally gets more action on a full-size largemouth lure, a 6-inch lizard.

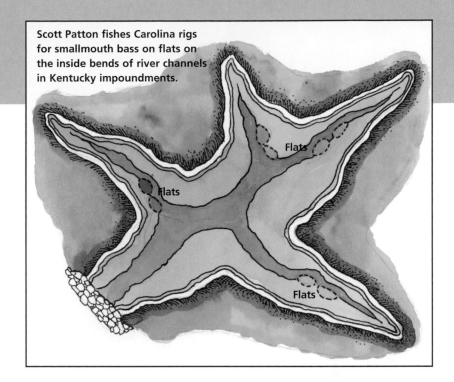

Scott Patton fishes Carolina rigs for smallmouth bass on flats on the inside bends of river channels in Kentucky impoundments.

When he isn't fishing tournaments, Patton guides for smallmouth, largemouth and striped bass on Dale Hollow, Lake Cumberland, Kentucky Lake and other Bluegrass State reservoirs. On Dale Hollow, especially, a Carolina rigged lizard keeps his clients in touch with hard-fighting smallmouth.

"At Dale Hollow," says Patton, "we catch a lot of smallmouth on underwater weedbeds, both hydrilla and milfoil. I've seen the grass in water as deep as 15 feet. In the deeper water, it grows 3 to 4 feet tall. The bass relate to the grass in spring and again in fall. In the summer, they usually hold deeper than the grass grows."

Patton finds many productive grassbeds on flats near islands and on the inside turns of river bends. On Dale Hollow, many such bends exist up the Wolf River and on the main lake. Patton also catches smallmouth from flats on inside river bends on Lake Cumberland. These flats feature gravel bottoms but no weeds.

When fishing weeds with clients, Patton holds his boat within a cast of the vegetation, usually over 25 to 35 feet of water, depending on the degree of slope. His customers sling Carolina rigged lizards up into the weed edge and to clumps of weeds in 12 to 14 feet of water and work them back out. On many outings, the lizards draw strikes from both largemouth and smallmouth bass.

UP THE challenge of landing bronzebacks by using ultralight lines.

GO SUPERLIGHT FOR SMALLMOUTH

Battling bronzebacks on 2-pound line isn't for everybody. Some anglers couldn't stand the excitement

THOSE WHO HAVE EXPERIENCED IT claim that no thrill in bass fishing is equal to battling a big smallmouth on light tackle. To some, "light" is measured in 6- and 8-pound-test increments. To others, the term ultralight equates to 4- and even 2-pound test.

If you are up for the latter challenge, then read on. Most anglers who opt for 2-pound test are seeking record book catches in the line class. Others do it just to press the outer limits of the lightest tackle imaginable.

THE 2-POUND QUEST

Big fish on light line are nothing new to Tuscumbia, Ala., angler Steve Hacker. The Pickwick Lake guide has boated countless smallmouth over 6 pounds, and a few approaching 8, on 6-pound line. Hacker once held the International Game Fish Association (IGFA) 8-pound-class world record for a 69-pound, 8-ounce blue catfish he wrestled from Pickwick's current on 6-pound mono. Intrigued by the challenge and added sporting qualities of such a quest, he became captivated by the notion of beating big bronzebacks on 2-pound line.

"I have a cousin who loves fishing superlight line; he claims every fish you catch on it, regardless of how big, is an adventure," Hacker says. "I was always too afraid to use it at Pickwick, where there's always the potential of hanging a giant smallmouth. I figured as soon as I spooled up with 2-pound test, that's when that 10-pounder would hit."

Whatever spinning rod you select for superlight smallmouth fishing, Hacker suggests keeping these pointers in mind: "Forget a fast action rod, the kind you might use with 6- or 8-pound test when fishing grubs in clear water. A fast-tipped rod won't

(Opposite page) PICKWICK LAKE guide Steve Hacker finds superlight tackle challenging and fun.

Soft Plastic Tip

If you're fishing tiny lures on 2-pound-test line and hook a feisty smallmouth, you're better off fighting the fish with the rod instead of the reel drag. Keep the drag extremely light so if a fish does max out the rod, the line will slip. Backreeling is also a possibility, but unless you're very good at it, the experts don't recommend trying to backreel a big smallie on superlight line.

flex enough when you're using 2-pound line. Your rod must be capable of absorbing most of the shock of a big smallie's strike and powerful runs. The Loomis 720 blank is an excellent choice because it has a progressive, light power action that seems perfect for soaking up stress without transferring too much to that wispy line."

By now you're asking, "How do you set the hook with an extremely light rod?" When using 2-pound line — you don't!

"Whether I'm using a tiny lure or a live minnow for bait, I just pull the rod to the side slightly to set the hook. Never, never use a sharp, overhead snap-set with superlight line," Hacker cautions.

"Obviously you have to check your line for rough spots or nicks after nearly every cast," He warns. "Smallmouth love rocky areas, and even the most insignificant abrasion can end up with your line parting when you're fighting a big smallie."

Although a reel with a smooth drag is needed, Hacker tries to avoid relying on the drag when fighting a fish, often a difficult task in heavy river current.

For superlight fishing, Hacker recommends single-hook lures, such as jigs.

"Your lure will sink faster on 2-pound line, allowing you to downsize to a 1/16-ounce jig," he says. "Avoid lures heavier than 1/8 ounce. Anything heavier than that is too hard to work properly with a light rod. A jig is a 'feel' bait, and that's another reason I like the Loomis 720 blank — it's light, but it's still powerful and sensitive. You don't want a buggy whip for smallies."

Live bait requires a smaller hook; Hacker likes the Gamakatsu Octopus bait hook in No. 4 or No. 2 size with a fresh-caught threadfin shad. Other suitable superlight baits include small golden shiners or "tuffy" minnows.

If you've had any experience with light line, you're probably wondering how to tie the jig or hook to that whisper-thin line.

"I had never used a leader or snelled hook before I started toying with superlight bassin'," Hacker admits. "But these rigs make a lot of sense with 2-pound line."

European Alternative

Superlight fishing isn't an oddity in Europe — it's the norm. Relatively little water, combined with a dense population, makes gamefish on this continent so line-shy that lines testing well under 2 pounds are commonly employed.

Few Americans are more familiar with European tackle and techniques than Randall Akin. The Claremore, Okla., fishing enthusiast has fished in European match competitions as a member of the United States match fishing team; he's currently involved in the sales and distribution of European tackle stateside.

"The lightest line I've used had a breaking strength of 6 ounces, and the smallest hook was a No. 30 — about as big as a question mark on a typewriter," Akin says.

"In European tackle, it's the rod, not the line, that handles most of the shock from a fighting fish," he says. "A 12- or 14-foot float rod can be bent double without stressing the line at the reel. That's the Europeans' secret of fighting big fish on amazingly light line. The rod literally wears them out. It absorbs the power of a strong fish, be it a trout, pike or smallmouth, like nothing else can."

Akin says European tackle and techniques aren't well-suited to a traditional bass fishing approach.

"Most bass anglers rely on their boat to get them to the fish, while in Europe, few fishermen have boats, so they devise ways to bring the fish to them. They've refined bank fishing to an art. Most fishing

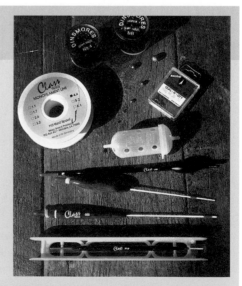

is done by 'feeding' (chumming) live bait, usually maggots, which draws the fish to the fisherman."

SPIDER-WEB-THIN lines and big smallies are an exciting combination. Plenty of patience and a rod that absorbs most of the shock of these fighters are required.

IGFA rules permit the use of a double line or leader, provided the length of either is limited to 6 feet. If a 2-pound main line is used in conjunction with, for example, a 6-pound leader, the breaking strength of the main line, not the leader, is taken into account for record-book purposes.

"When using jigs, I manufacture a leader by taking 12 to 18 inches of 6-pound line and tying a Uni-Knot in one end, without pulling the loop all the way closed," he explains. "I attach the 2-pound main line to the loop with either a second Uni-Knot or a Palomar knot. The jig is then tied to the end of the 6-pound leader with a Uni-Knot."

Hacker takes an easier route when fishing live minnows. "I use light snell rigs, consisting of a small hook tied to a short leader," he says. "These are very handy when bait-fishing around rocks, because you can re-rig quickly should you break off." When weight is needed, Hacker pinches a small split shot to the leader's loop. "Never pinch a split shot onto 2-pound line," he warns.

DOING BATTLE

Now that you're rigged and ready for superlight smallmouth fishing, it's time to do battle with a big bronzeback. Choosing the right places to fish is as important as fishing at the right time.

"You need to steer clear of snag-infested waters, obviously," he says. "But this won't hurt you when hunting fish, because smallies don't like thick cover all that much anyway. I'll usually hunt them on offshore humps, shell mounds or rockpiles."

Hacker lets the bass bite dictate when to break out the superlight gear. "I'm on the water almost every day, so when the big fish bite gets going, I can't resist trying the 2-pound stuff, especially if I'm on one of the many big, slick humps at Pick-wick," he says.

Once Hacker succeeds in getting a big smallie to bite, he employs some specialized techniques to keep that spider web line from snapping.

"The first rule is to keep the fish away from the boat as long as possible — not that you'll have much to say about it anyway," he says with a laugh. "Experienced smallmouth anglers cringe when they see somebody reel a big bronzeback up to the boat, only to lose it when it makes a last-minute dive for deep water. You'll lose a big one with 10-, even 15-pound line if you try to bring it in when it's fresh. Play the fish for as long as you can. Make sure it's well-worn out before attempting to bring it to the boat."

Hacker again stresses the importance of using the rod, not the reel, to fight the fish.

"I keep the rod high and have the drag set so it slips as soon as the rod is loaded up by the fish's run." Never be in a hurry, he emphasizes. "The only real reason to use 2-pound line is to enjoy the fight, so don't try to rush things. Two-pound line is only half as strong as 4, but it may take six times as long to land a fish when using it."

When fighting a big smallie in moving water, pay attention to where your boat is drifting, Steve warns. "I look around me to see if I'm drifting toward a buoy or some other obstruction, and correct the drift well ahead of time with the trolling motor. In extremely fast current, it may not be necessary for you to crank up the big motor with one hand while you're hangin' on to the rod with the other."

Expect a lot of "jumpin' and carryin' on" from a smallie hooked on superlight line.

"You're going to lose some when they jump, but that's to be expected with line this light," he says. "I've had several really big fish on that I haven't been able to handle, but I'm not giving up. Those big fish are absolutely wild on 2-pound test; it's like they don't even know they're hooked."

SOFT JERKBAITS aren't just
for largemouth fishing.

SOFT SERVE SMALLIES

If you guess that soft jerkbaits are
primarily largemouth baits, then guess again

SMALLMOUTH FANS, prepare to have your eyes opened about soft jerkbaits! The following lesson includes insight from smallmouth experts who will offer sage advice into fishing these exciting and unusually productive lures for your favorite bass. Their tips on presentation and rigging are geared to help you boat more and bigger smallmouth, and have a ton of fun doing it!

WHY THEY WORK

The qualities that make a soft jerkbait a super largemouth lure make it a sensational smallmouth lure, says Herb Reed, an avid smallmouth fan and creator of the Slug-Go. "These lures have a simple, streamlined appearance and a random action that present a realistic impression of a disoriented baitfish," he explains.

Because soft jerkbaits lack the built-in repetitive action common to most bass lures, they appear far more lifelike in clear water. "And because smallmouth often favor clear water, they tend to bypass most artificials presented to them," Reed notes. "They can easily detect the flaws other lure types transmit, such as unrealistic wobbles or repetitive movements unlike those of living prey."

Thanks to their inherent simplicity, soft jerkbaits may be worked from top to bottom to cash in on smallmouth nearly all year long, according to Reed.

"You can rig them weightless and float them around shallow cover," he says. "You can skip them out of the water when smallies are chasing baitfish on top. And you can fish them right on the bottom, or hop them down ledges when these fish are deep. They're the most versatile smallmouth lures in your tacklebox."

STING 'EM

Adding a stinger hook to a Slug-Go or similar soft jerk lure is one sure way to catch more of the fish that bite, according to Herb Reed.

"At certain times of the year, especially right after the spawn, smallmouth have a tendency to butt the lure but not strike it," Reed explained. "This is when I'll go to a stinger hook."

Soft Plastic Tip

After the spawn, big smallmouth often congregate at the deeper ends of flats, where they may suspend and school up on baitfish. A Slug-Go or similar lure works great in the same places you'd normally tempt these postspawners with a large topwater, like a Zara Spook. In superclear water, experts prefer the 6-inch lures, which you can cast farther. Fish them on a stiff 6 1/2-foot spinning rod or medium action baitcaster with 10-pound line, and often rig a stinger hook to the lure.

DALE HOLLOW guide Mike Johnson fishes soft jerkbaits over flats and long points to tempt open water smallmouth.

When bass are offshore and cover isn't a factor, Reed adds a sharp No. 2 treble hook to the primary hook. Using a 6-inch Slug-Go, he runs the point of the primary hook first through the eye of the treble hook, then through and finally out of the worm, "tex-posing" it according to instructions on the package. The upward hook of the treble is then buried in the worm, while the other two hooks hang fully exposed.

"This will hook 'em if they even breathe on it," Reed quips. When smallies are hanging close to shallow cover, such as flooded bushes, but hesitant to engulf the lure completely, Reed will use a similar setup, substituting a spinnerbait trailer hook for the treble. Here, both the primary hook and the stinger are "tex-posed" to rest in the groove on top of the lure.

Reed recommends attaching the stinger hook to the primary hook, by a snell made from monofilament, and not separating the two. This will keep both hooks straight and increase your odds of boating a big fish.

The Weighting Game

Not enough smallmouth anglers have experimented with weighting their soft jerkbaits, Herb Reed believes. "These baits have gained the reputation of being visual lures, but they are highly effective when fished deeper," he advises. Varying the number and placement of the nail-like insert weights made for use with soft jerks, the angler can exercise almost total control over the speed and trajectory at which the lure sinks.

"By placing the weights sideways through the middle of the lure, you can make the bait fall almost horizontally, which is highly effective when smallmouth are suspended beneath a cloud of bait-

fish," Reed indicated.

"Then again, by concentrating the weights at the head, you can get the lure to fall quickly to the bottom, where you can dead-jump it for deeper smallies."

Reed's dead-jumping technique is one that can be used whenever smallmouth are deep.

"First of all, remember that you can't fish the lure as quickly as you might in shallow water," Reed said. "When you re-

move the visual element, fishing a soft jerkbait becomes a touchy-feely experience. You may not know when a fish takes the lure in deep water, so you've got to take your time."

After casting the weighted lure to deep structure, allow it to fall on a tight line, then reel up any slack very slowly until you barely feel the weight of the bait, Reed recommends. "Give one sharp jerk with the rod tip and the bait will jump off the bottom. Let the line go slack so the lure can gyrate and dive erratically as it falls. Then reel up the slack very slowly, feeling as you go. If you detect a fish, set the hook hard. The strike usually comes on the fall."

GUIDING ANCESTORS

Ancestors play an important role in world mythology. For the Australian Aborigines, the laws and customs established by ancestor spirits (left) act as guidelines for life today. These ancestors exist outside time, in the eternal present of the Dreamtime. Aboriginal myths are stories of the Dreamtime, and Aboriginal art and ceremonies are ways of connecting with the ancestors.

CHALLENGING THE GODS

Not all are content to worship the gods; some even challenge them. When Nimrod, King of Babylon, built a tower to reach heaven and make war on God, God sent 70 angels to confuse the builders' tongues. Some say that this is why people now speak different languages.

The Tower of Babel fell when the workmen could no longer understand each other

STORYTELLING

Myths are passed on by storytelling, not only by word of mouth and in writing, but also in rituals, dances, dramas, and artworks. This *Medicine Beaver* mask tells the story of the life-or-death struggle between a North American Nisga-a shaman, or medicine man, and a giant beaver, in which the shaman made the beaver into his spirit helper.

PERSEPHONE AND HADES

Many mythologies hope for a new life after death. The Egyptians and the Greeks both linked the idea of an afterlife with the annual death and resurrection of wheat. The Greeks worshiped Persephone, daughter of the wheat goddess Demeter, as queen of the dead, in rites that they believed held the entire human race together.

1,000 B.C.E.					1 C.E.		1,000 C.E.
Hindu figure of Garuda	Bible story of Adam and Eve	Polynesian god Tangaroa	Greek supreme god Zeus	Celtic horned god Cernunnos	Roman war god Mars	Norse god Thor's hammer	Japanese prayer offerings

Creation of the world

COSMIC EGG
A bird-man from Rapa Nui (Easter Island) is shown holding the cosmic egg that contains the world. Each year in the nesting season, the man whose servant was the first to gather an egg became Rapa Nui's Bird Man, the living representative for that year of the creator god Makemake.

MANY PEOPLES seem to agree that this world was made as a deliberate act of creation by a divine being. Often the world is described as having originally been all ocean, and it is from the sea that the world emerges in the earliest mythologies. Nun was the god of the Egyptian primal ocean. The Arctic Tikigak people say that Raven made the land by harpooning a great whale, which then floated and became dry land. Sometimes there are two creators, who together shape the world, such as First Creator and Lone Man of the Native American Mandan tribe. They sent a mud hen down to fetch mud from the bottom of the flood to make the first land.

FIRE AND ICE
The Vikings believed that the world began when fire from the south met ice from the north. At the center, the ice began to thaw and, as it dripped, it shaped itself into the first being, Ymir, whose sweat formed the first frost giants. Then the ice-melt shaped a cow, whose milk fed Ymir. As the cow licked the ice, she shaped the first man, Buri.

Pottery figurine of Gaea from Thebes, 450 B.C.

FLOATING DISK
According to the ancient Greeks, the first to be born from the primeval chaos was Gaea, the Earth. The Earth was conceived as a disk floating on a waste of waters, and encircled by the river Oceanus. Gaea gave birth to Uranus, the sky, and Cronus (time).

Ahura Mazda, from the tree of life relief, 9th century B.C.

THE BIG BANG
Scientists now say that the world began with the Big Bang, a huge explosion 13 billion years ago that sent matter in all directions to create the ever-expanding Universe. This is a new vision of beginning; a new "myth" for a scientific age.

CREATED FROM GOODNESS
The ancient Persians believed in twin spirits who had existed since the beginning of time: Ahura Mazda, who was good; and Ahriman, who was evil. It was Ahura Mazda who created the physical world, set time in motion, and created humankind.

TURTLE ISLAND
Many Native Americans believe that this world is supported on a turtle's back. According to the Seneca tribe, when the first woman fell down from another world in the sky, the toad that lived on the primal waters dived down to fetch mud to place on the turtle's back. The mud, which became Earth, provided support for the first woman.

The first land was said to have been created on a turtle's back

19th-century Native American Cheyenne shield

CURDLING OCEAN
The Japanese god Izanagi and his wife Izanami stood on the floating bridge of heaven and stirred the ocean with a jeweled spear until it curdled and formed the first island, Onokoro. They built a house there, with a central stone pillar that is the backbone of the world.

Vishnu sits on top of Mount Mandara

OCEAN CHURNING
At the beginning of this cycle of creation, a number of vital treasures, including the elixir of immortality, were not to be found, so the Hindu gods decided to churn the ocean, using Mount Mandara as the paddle. As they churned, the ocean turned to milk, then to butter, and the Sun and Moon arose. As they churned some more, the elixir was finally created.

Vasuki, the cosmic serpent, was used as a rope to twist the mountain

The mountain is supported by a giant turtle

The Milky Way and the planets of the Solar System. Clockwise from the bottom are the Earth, Mars, Jupiter, Saturn, Uranus, and Neptune.

11

The cosmos

PEOPLE HAVE ALWAYS WONDERED about the mysteries of the world, from its origin and shape to its cosmos, or order. The world is often thought to have emerged from a cosmic egg. In China, the warring forces of yin and yang in the egg created the first being, Pan Gu. The Dogon of West Africa believe the world was formed from a vibrating egg that burst open to reveal a creator spirit. The Ainu of Japan believed there were six skies above this Earth and six worlds below it, the abodes of gods, demons, and animals. The world has long been thought of as round. A myth told by the Inuit people of the Arctic tundra tells how two families set out in opposite directions to discover how big the world is. When they met up again, they were very old, but the fact that they came back to where they started proved that the world is round. The Mangaian people of Polynesia say that the universe is held in the shell of a huge coconut.

Bradma, the creator of the Universe, is shown on Vishnu's forehead

Vishnu's conch shell symbolizes the very first vibration of the Universe — the sound "om"

The discus symbolizes the mind and the sun

WORLD IN A SEALSKIN
On this sealskin painted by the Chukchi people of Siberia, the whole Arctic world – Sun, Moon, land, sea, and sky – is captured in a small space. Human beings share creation with spirits, animals, and gods such as the creator Raven and his wife, Miti, and Sedna, the mother of the sea beasts.

Inuit people of the Arctic tundra build an igloo, which is round like the world

YIN AND YANG
The Chinese believed that the first being, Pan Gu, was created inside a cosmic egg by the opposing forces of yin and yang. When at last the conflict between yin and yang broke the egg open, Pan Gu was born and pushed the sky away from the Earth. After he died, exhausted by this labor, his body formed the mountains and the land — and his fleas became humankind.

Yin and yang symbolize universal opposites, such as good and evil, that must be equally balanced for a harmonious world

WORLD TREE
For the Vikings the nine worlds, including humankind's "middle Earth," were arranged in three layers around the huge ash tree Yggdrasil, which stands at the center of the cosmos. The Vikings believed that the worlds of gods, giants, elves, dwarfs, humans, and the dead were all sustained by the world tree.

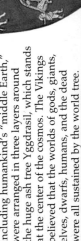

COSMIC STONE

This Babylonian boundary stone shows the gods and goddesses of the Babylonian cosmos as witnesses to a legal agreement. At the top are symbols of the goddess of love and war Ishtar, the moon god Sin, and the Sun god Shamash. An underworld snake wriggles up the side. The scorpion in the center row is the symbol of Ishhara, the goddess of marriage and childbirth and enforcer of oaths.

Sin, the moon god, is represented by a crescent moon

This symbol for the planet Venus represents Ishtar, goddess of love and fertility

Vishnu's lotus flower is a symbol of purity

NUT AND GEB

The ancient Egyptians thought that the Earth was male, personified by the Earth god Geb, and that Geb mated with his sister Nut, the sky, to produce the stars. Nut and Geb were wrenched apart by their father Shu, god of the air, who holds Nut aloft and pins Geb down with his feet.

Each night the sun god Ra is swallowed by Nut, to be born again next morning

Underworld snakes writhe in the lowest region of the cosmos, Tala, where murderers are reborn

This golden mace is a symbol of knowledge

PAPA AND RANGI

The Maoris tell how Papa, the Earth goddess, coupled with Rangi, the sky god. So closely did Papa and Rangi cling to each other that their children could not leave the Earth womb. Eventually, Papa and Rangi were forced apart by one of their children, Tane, the forest god.

Watchful eyes of the owl Koururu, sacrificed by Rongo, god of agriculture, to protect his house

Varuna, god of the waters, sits on an imaginary beast

This carving stood at the entrance to a Maori assembly house on North Island, New Zealand

VISHNU'S WORLD

Vishnu the preserver is one of the three great gods of the Hindu religion. At the end of each cycle of creation, Vishnu sleeps on the world serpent Shesha, preserving the seed of a new creation that will rise when he wakes. When Vishnu was incarnated as the hero Krishna, his mother looked into his mouth and saw the whole universe. This 19th-century painting shows Vishnu as the universe.

Sun and Moon

THE SUN AND THE MOON, which light up the sky by day and night and enable us to tell the time, have been the subject of many myths. For the Native American Zuni people, Moonlight-Giving Mother and Sun Father are the givers of light and life. The Native American Cherokees say the sun is female and tell of her grief when her daughter died from a rattlesnake bite. Sun hid herself away, the world grew dark, and her tears caused a flood. Only the dancing and singing of young men and women could cheer her up. The Arctic Chukchi tell how a woman married the sun, but a black beetle took her place; it was only when her son sought out his father that the imposter was discovered. Another Chukchi woman married the moon; she had been deserted by her husband and left to starve, but she crawled to moon's house and became his wife.

DEALER OF DAYS
The moon god Thoth was in charge of the Egyptian calendar, which had 12 months with 30 days each. The sky goddess Nut, who had been cursed so that she could never give birth, won five extra days from Thoth in which she had her children.

THE ROMAN GODDESS DIANA
Diana (Artemis in Greek) is shown here with her foot resting on the Moon, with which she was closely associated. More often, however, she is depicted with a crescent Moon in her hair.

Diana as a crowned moon goddess

The face on this Inuit mask represents the spirit of the moon

Decorative feathers represent the stars

White border around the face symbolizes air

Native American Haida mask

Painted moon face sculpted in wood

FEEDING HUMANKIND
The Inuit moon man is called Igaluk or Tarqeq. Shamans make spirit journeys to ask him to promise that he will send animals for men to hunt. The moon man also helps the souls of the dead to be reborn as humans, animals, or fish.

POLLUTING THE WORLD
A Native American Haida myth tells how Wultcixaiya, the son of the moon, rescued his sister from her unhappy marriage to Pestilence. Wearing a steel coat, he broke into Pestilence's house of rock, freeing her, but also polluting the world with sickness and disease.

SUN GOD RA
The falcon-headed god Horus joined forces with the Egyptian Sun god Ra and became Ra-Horakhty. He sailed a special boat, the *Solar Barque*, across the sky by day and through the underworld by night.

The Sun's rays beam down on a worshiper

Projections symbolize the Sun's rays

INCA INTI
Viracocha, the Inca creator god, ordered the Sun, Moon, and stars to emerge from the Island of the Sun, in Lake Titicaca, to bring light to the world. Inti, the Sun god, was regarded as the father of the Inca emperors, and his wife, Mama Kilya, the moon goddess, as the mother of the Inca race.

Pre-Columbian gold sun mask, 300 B.C.E

CHILDREN OF THE SUN
The Native American Tsimshian hero Asdiwal was a great hunter, who pursued a bear right up to the sky. The bear turned out to be the Sun's beautiful daughter, whom Asdiwal married. The Sun also has a son, a shining prince of the sky, who had a constant battle of wits with his cheeky servant.

Tsimshian chief's ceremonial headdress representing the Sun

The fertility goddess Ishtar

Ea, the water god

Shamash rising between two mountains

Amaterasu holds the imperial sword and necklace

ENEMY OF DARKNESS
The Babylonian Sun god Shamash was the only being able to cross the ocean of death, until the hero Gilgamesh. Shamash was a lawgiver and healer, the enemy of darkness, wrongdoing, and disease.

SUN GODDESS AMATERASU
The Japanese Sun goddess Amaterasu was so offended by her brother Susano's practical jokes that she hid in a cave and deprived the world of the Sun. Uzume, the goddess of mirth, did a striptease and made the other gods laugh. Intrigued, Amaterasu emerged from the cave, returning sunlight to the world.

Making humankind

ALL MYTHOLOGIES TELL how the first human beings were made. Often the creator shaped them from clay or mud. The Unalit (North Alaskan Inuit) say that the first man was born from the pod of a beach pea. When he burst out of the pod, he was met by Raven, who taught him how to live and made him a wife out of clay. The Egyptians believed that the first human beings were made from the tears of Ra, the sun god. For the Serbians, people were made from the creator's sweat, which is why they say we are doomed to a life of toil. The Norse god Odin made the first man and woman from driftwood, but there is also a myth telling how the Norse god Heimdall fathered the various kinds of men: serfs, warriors, and kings.

Brahma has four heads so that he can see in all directions

Tangaroa brings forth other beings

Wooden statue from the Tubuaï Islands in Polynesia, where the supreme god Tangaroa is called A'a

BRAHMA THE CREATOR
The Hindu creator Brahma is the universal soul, the "self-existent great-grandfather." He made the world and everything in it. He is sometimes called Purusha, the first being. As Purusha he divided himself into two, male and female, and coupled in the form of every creature, from humans to ants.

Carved wooden bowl from the Yoruba in West Africa

The cosmic serpent Aido-Hwedo coiled itself around the Earth

BODIES OF CLAY
The West African creator Mawu made the first people from clay and water. The first man and woman, sometimes called Adanhu and Yewa, were sent down from the sky with the rainbow serpent Aido-Hwedo. For the first 17 days it did nothing but rain; the man and woman did not speak but only called out the name of the god who had sent them to Earth.

Adanhu

Yewa

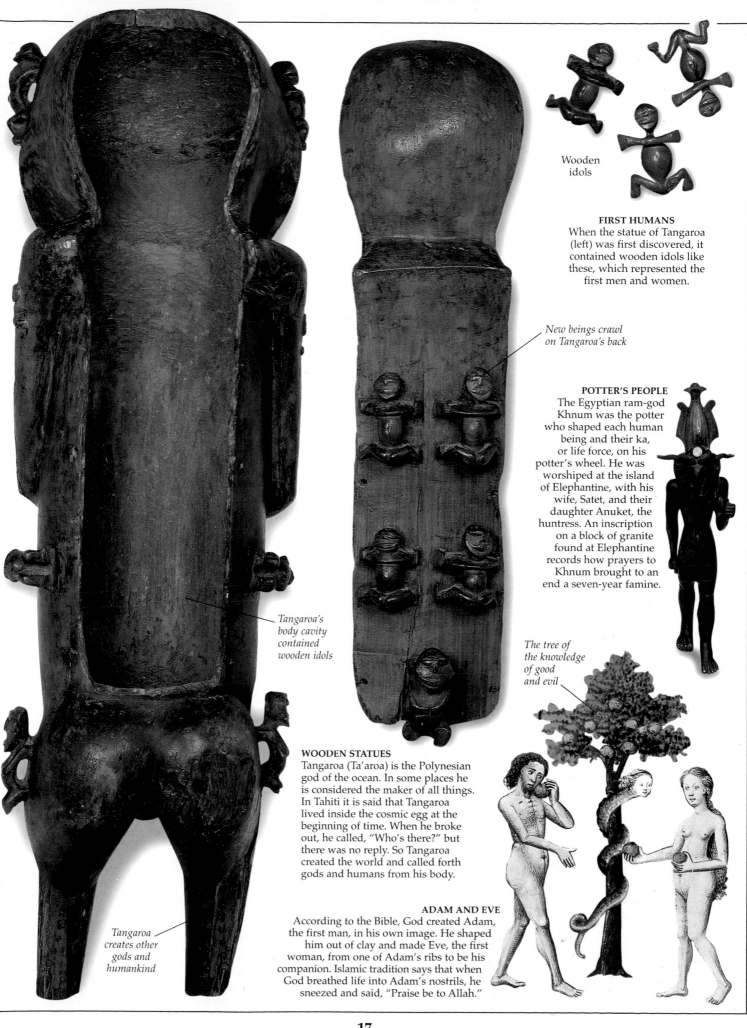

Wooden idols

FIRST HUMANS
When the statue of Tangaroa (left) was first discovered, it contained wooden idols like these, which represented the first men and women.

New beings crawl on Tangaroa's back

POTTER'S PEOPLE
The Egyptian ram-god Khnum was the potter who shaped each human being and their ka, or life force, on his potter's wheel. He was worshiped at the island of Elephantine, with his wife, Satet, and their daughter Anuket, the huntress. An inscription on a block of granite found at Elephantine records how prayers to Khnum brought to an end a seven-year famine.

Tangaroa's body cavity contained wooden idols

The tree of the knowledge of good and evil

WOODEN STATUES
Tangaroa (Ta'aroa) is the Polynesian god of the ocean. In some places he is considered the maker of all things. In Tahiti it is said that Tangaroa lived inside the cosmic egg at the beginning of time. When he broke out, he called, "Who's there?" but there was no reply. So Tangaroa created the world and called forth gods and humans from his body.

Tangaroa creates other gods and humankind

ADAM AND EVE
According to the Bible, God created Adam, the first man, in his own image. He shaped him out of clay and made Eve, the first woman, from one of Adam's ribs to be his companion. Islamic tradition says that when God breathed life into Adam's nostrils, he sneezed and said, "Praise be to Allah."

Supreme beings

MOST MYTHOLOGIES tell of one god who reigns supreme over all others. These supreme gods may be associated with the creation of the world and humankind. Many supreme deities, such as the Greek god Zeus, are essentially sky gods; others may be Sun, battle, city, or tribal gods. In some cultures, especially in Africa, the supreme god is thought to have retired from the world after the initial creation. This is the case with Nana-Buluku, the creator deity of the Fon of West Africa; and with Nyame of the West African Ashanti people. Over time such gods may be almost forgotten. For instance, Nana-Buluku's daughter Mawu is now routinely described as the creator, and the word "mawu" has come to mean "god" in Fon.

Thunderbolts were made for Zeus by the Cyclopes, giants who helped in the war against Zeus's father

RULER OF THE GREEKS
Zeus (known as Jupiter to the Romans) was ruler of the Greek gods. Zeus overthrew his father, Cronos, before establishing his rule on Mount Olympus. His wife, Hera, goddess of marriage, was jealous because of his many love affairs, during which he fathered the gods Apollo and Artemis, and the heroes Perseus and Heracles (or Hercules).

Made of bronze and decorated with silver, this late Bronze Age figure represents the storm god Baal

THE RAINMAKER
The Canaanite storm god Baal made thunder with his mace and produced lightning from his lance. Baal revolted against El, his father, by defeating El's favorite, Yam, the god of the sea. Another myth tells of his long battle against Mot, god of death.

BABYLONIAN KING OF THE GODS
This doglike dragon is the symbol of Marduk, the Babylonian king of the gods. Strong and heroic, he was given authority over the other gods, including his father, Ea, the god of wisdom, when he agreed to slay the dragon Tiamat (one of two primal beings). Marduk created humankind from the blood of Tiamat's son Kingu.

The feathers of more than 250 quetzal birds make up this headdress

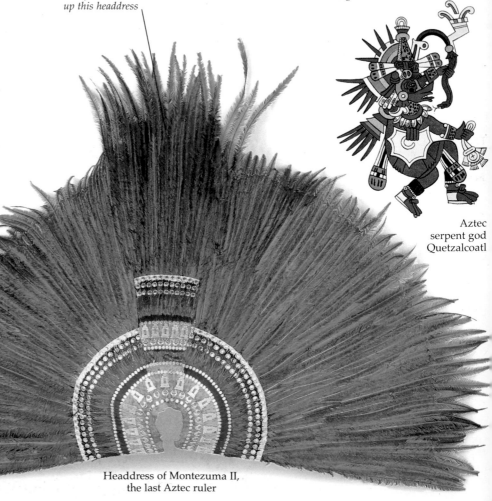

Aztec serpent god Quetzalcoatl

FEATHERED SERPENT
Half-snake, half-bird, Quetzalcoatl was the Aztec lord of life and god of the winds. He descended to the underworld to retrieve the bones of early humans in order to create new beings. The underworld was ruled by his father, the death god Mictlantecuhtli.

Headdress of Montezuma II, the last Aztec ruler

Wooden kantele from Karelia in Finland, 1893

Stoneware Taoist shrine of the Ming dynasty, 1406 A.D.

Lao-tzu, the founder of Taoism, is shown riding a buffalo

SINGING SHAMAN
Vainamoinen, the eternal singer, was the son of the Finnish air-goddess Ilmatar. He was born old, so no one wanted to marry him — one girl, Aino, even became a mermaid rather than be his bride. Vainamoinen was a shaman, whose songs to the sound of his harplike kantele were acts of creative magic.

The Jade Emperor

LORD OF THE HEAVENS
The Chinese gods formed a huge bureaucracy, at the head of which was the Jade Emperor. He was assisted by the God of the Eastern Peak, who had no fewer than 75 departments under his control, each supervised by lesser gods. The Jade Emperor's wife was Xi Wang Mu, the Queen Mother of the West, guardian of the peaches of immortality, which she served at a great feast once every 1,000 years.

Ebony mortar and pestle from Tanzania, East Africa

Mortar   *Pestle*

The God of the Eastern Peak

STAIRWAY TO HEAVEN
Nyame is the sky god of the Ashanti of Africa. He used to live close to humans, but when an old woman annoyed him by knocking him with her pestle as she pounded yams, he moved away toward the heavens. The old woman and her sons tried to reach him by piling mortars on top of each other, but they were one short. They took the mortar from the bottom to place it on the top, and the pile collapsed, killing them all.

19

Scary monsters

Giants are found throughout mythology. Their size makes them terrifying, but often they are portrayed as slow, stupid, and easily outwitted, like the Cyclops Polyphemus, who believes that the hero Odysseus's name is Nobody and yells out "Nobody is hurting me" when Odysseus blinds him. Many of the first beings were monsters, such as Ymir, the Norse frost giant.

Cyclopes had only one eye

Fierce incisors tear meat from the bone

ONE-EYED OGRE
Polyphemus was one of the legendary Cyclopes, one-eyed giants with ferocious appetites. He was blinded by Odysseus, who plunged a red-hot stake into his eye. But Polyphemus's father, Poseidon, was so enraged that he persecuted Odysseus — wrecking his ships, drowning his crews, and keeping him from his home for ten long years.

Skulls of mastodons (extinct elephant-like mammals) were once believed to be Cyclopes' skulls

Greedy Cyclopes could devour whole carcasses at one sitting

Tunic made from the hides of the Cyclops's prey

Cyclopes tore their prey limb from limb

Ancestor worship

In MANY CULTURES, FEAR OF THE EVIL POWER of spirits of the dead is balanced by a belief in the protective power of the spirits of ancestors, who are believed to watch over and guide the living. For this reason offerings may be made to ancestors' shrines. For instance, in China the head of a family must make regular sacrifices of food at the graves of his ancestors; if not, the "hungry ghosts" may cause trouble. In both China and Japan, wooden tablets inscribed with the names of ancestors are kept in a household shrine. The duty that the living owe to the dead was never more pressing than in ancient Egypt, where it was vital that the eldest living son of deceased parents raise a monument to their memory and pronounce their names every time he passed it, to keep their names alive.

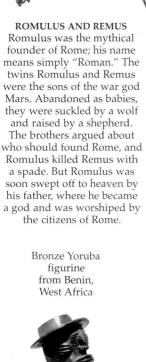

ROMULUS AND REMUS
Romulus was the mythical founder of Rome; his name means simply "Roman." The twins Romulus and Remus were the sons of the war god Mars. Abandoned as babies, they were suckled by a wolf and raised by a shepherd. The brothers argued about who should found Rome, and Romulus killed Remus with a spade. But Romulus was soon swept off to heaven by his father, where he became a god and was worshiped by the citizens of Rome.

Bronze Yoruba figurine from Benin, West Africa

Female figure from Middle Sepik River, Papua New Guinea

Procession of Oshun's devotees

OSHUN WORSHIP
Ancestors are worshiped in many parts of Africa and are prayed to for good health, fertility, and good fortune. The Yoruba people of West Africa worship Oshun, goddess of the river that bears the same name. Oshun was married to the thunder god Shango and has human descendants. People bathe in the Oshun River to protect themselves from disease. Women, in particular, consult the goddess Oshun in cases of family problems or illness.

LIFE-GIVING ANCESTORS
In New Guinea, carved figures of ancestors were present at *moguru* (life-giving ceremonies) at which the young were initiated into adulthood and the men gained prowess as fighters. In the Papuan Gulf, the fierce Kerua headhunters hung human skulls from carved boards as offerings to ancestral beings.

COLOSSAL CHIEFS
On Rapa Nui (Easter Island), a remote and barren island of volcanic rock stranded in the eastern Pacific, stand hundreds of monolithic stone figures. They are *moai* – figures of dead chiefs who were regarded as descendants of the gods.

FEAST OF LANTERNS
The *bon* festival, held in Japan each July, is known as the Feast of Lanterns. It is held in honor of the spirits of the dead, which return to Earth for the three days of the festival. Relatives of the deceased pray at shrines, where they leave food and other treats for the spirits to feast on.

DREAMTIME ANCESTORS
The Dreamtime is the eternal present in which the revered ancestors of the Australian Aborigines exist, constantly creating the world. Creation story designs, shown to the Aborigines by the ancestors, are still painted on bodies, rocks, and bark, as in the painting (left) from Arnhem Land, North Australia. Aborigines carve pictures showing events in the Dreamtime on sacred wooden and stone artifacts, called *churinga*. These objects embody ancestral spiritual power and must not be seen by women or the uninitiated.

Aboriginal stone knife similar to those used by the eternal ancestors to create humans

Bark sheath

Papuan ancestral tablet, or ceremonial board

Gap-toothed Louhi as an eagle-woman with scythe-like claws

Evil forces

BESIDES GODS OF DEATH and sterility, there are many demons and forces of evil in world mythology. Balanced against these are forces of good which came into being to rid the world of evil. In Siberia it is told how the creator Ulgan made himself a companion, Erlik, from mud floating on the primal ocean. But Erlik, jealous of Ulgan, saved mud to try to build his own world, and he breathed life into humankind without Ulgan's permission. For these betrayals, Erlik was banished to the underworld, where he sits surrounded by evil spirits. Evil beings are very active in Hindu mythology, which has many antigods and demons. One of the most fearsome of all evil spirits is Vucub-Caquix, the Mayan monster macaw who claimed to be both the sun and the moon. He was killed in a terrible battle by the hero twins Hunahpu and Xbalanque, though not before he had torn off Hunahpu's arm.

WICKED LOUHI
The Finnish hag Louhi promised the smith Ilmarinen her daughter in return for the Sampo — a magic mill that grinds out grain, salt, and money. But Louhi proved treacherous, so Ilmarinen stole back the Sampo and set sail. Louhi turned into a bird and attacked the boat. In the struggle, the Sampo fell to the bottom of the sea, where it still grinds out salt to this day.

TREACHEROUS TRICKSTER
Loki, the Norse trickster god, turned against the other gods and brought about the death of Balder the Beautiful, son of the god Odin. For this, he is bound in agony, with poison dripping onto his face, until the final battle of Ragnarok, when he will lead an army from Hel against the gods in a ship made from dead men's nails.

Vajrapani holds a thunderbolt in his right hand

Tibetan statue of Vajrapani in his "ferocious" form

Fiery headdress encrusted with turquoise

DESTROYER OF EVIL
The Tibetan Vajrapani destroys the wicked with his *vajra* (thunderbolt), which spits lightning. One of eight main bodhisattvas, or Buddhist saints, Vajrapani shares characteristics with Indra, the Hindu god of the skies.

Vajrapani, wielder of the thunderbolt, is a symbol of law and order

Baba Yaga uses her pestle to stir up storms and spread disease

CANNIBAL WITCH
Baba Yaga is the cannibal witch of Russian myth. She lives in a revolving hut supported by hen's feet, and travels through the air in a mortar. Her male equivalent is Koshchei the Deathless, who abducts maidens and can turn into a dragon.

SULKY SUSANO
While bathing, the Japanese god Izanagi gave birth to three powerful divinities: the sun goddess Amaterasu, moon god Tsuki-Yomi, and Susano, the god of storms and chaos. Susano was meant to rule the sea, but he threw a tantrum and said he would rather go to the underworld. He flung a skinned horse into Amaterasu's sacred weaving hall, so was banished to Earth. There he rescued Kusa-nada-hime, the Rice Paddy Princess, from an eight-headed dragon, and made her his wife.

Text from a 19th-century print of the storm god Susano and his wife

Rice Paddy Princess Kusa-nada-hime

FIRST HUMAN SACRIFICE
When the Aztec goddess Coatlicue was pregnant with the supreme god Huitzilopochtli, she was attacked and murdered by her jealous daughter, Coyolxauhqui, and Coyolxauhqui's 400 brothers. But Huitzilopochtli leaped fully formed from his mother's decapitated body and slew his sister, making her the first human sacrifice.

Each of Durga's ten hands holds a special weapon — a symbol of divine power

INVINCIBLE DURGA
The Hindu warrior goddess Durga was one of the guises of the great goddess Devi. Durga was created to fight the *asuras* (demon enemies of the gods), who had conquered heaven. In each of her ten hands Durga holds a special weapon that she used to cut off the head of the buffalo-king of the *asuras*.

Susano, the Japanese storm god

Superheroes

MEN AND WOMEN WHO PERFORM great feats of daring and courage are celebrated in all mythologies. Often, they are said to be the children of gods or to be specially favored by the gods. Some heroes can defeat a whole series of enemies in single combat and rid countries of the monsters that plague them. Others, such as Hiawatha, are celebrated as peacemakers rather than as warriors. A typical hero is the Tibetan Gesar, who was a god chosen to be born as a man to rid the world of demons. Gesar became a powerful warrior king, with an immortal horse that flew through the sky and spoke all languages. At the end of his life, Gesar retired to heaven, but one day he will return, for evil can never be wholly defeated.

Polynices's corpse is left to rot

BRAVE ANTIGONE
Antigone was the daughter of Oedipus, king of Thebes in Greece. After his death, his two sons, Eteocles and Polynices, fought over the throne and killed each other. Their uncle Creon buried Eteocles with honor but threw the body of Polynices out to rot, regarding him as a traitor. Although threatened with death, Antigone bravely defied her uncle and gave Polynices a token burial, sprinkling three handfuls of dust over the corpse. Creon then walled her up in a cave without food or water, so she hanged herself.

When Krishna plays his magic flute, women within earshot join him to dance

Krishna is always blue, which shows that he is an incarnation of Vishnu

Krishna stands on a lotus flower, symbol of the earth

North American Indians made wampum (bead) belts to mark peace agreements

Beads are made from white and purple clam shells

DEMON DODGER
Krishna is the eighth avatar (incarnation) of the Hindu god Vishnu and is worshiped as a god in his own right. When he was a child, his mother took him to the countryside to escape the demon king Kansa, who was persecuting them. Kansa sent a female demon to poison him, but Krishna sucked the life out of her instead.

PEACEMAKER
Dekanah-wida was born to bring tidings of peace from the chief of the Sky Spirits to five warring Native American Indian tribes. Dekanah-wida made the Mohawk chief, Hiawatha, his peacemaker. Hiawatha then traveled between the tribes, persuading them to form the Iroquois League, whose members swore to live in peace together.

Sigurd kills the dragon

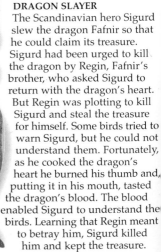

DRAGON SLAYER
The Scandinavian hero Sigurd slew the dragon Fafnir so that he could claim its treasure. Sigurd had been urged to kill the dragon by Regin, Fafnir's brother, who asked Sigurd to return with the dragon's heart. But Regin was plotting to kill Sigurd and steal the treasure for himself. Some birds tried to warn Sigurd, but he could not understand them. Fortunately, as he cooked the dragon's heart he burned his thumb and, putting it in his mouth, tasted the dragon's blood. The blood enabled Sigurd to understand the birds. Learning that Regin meant to betray him, Sigurd killed him and kept the treasure.

Fafnir the dragon

When Yi shot the suns, they fell to the Earth in the shape of crows

The Minotaur had a bull's head on a man's body

MONSTER KILLER
Theseus was the greatest of all Athenian heroes, said to be the son of the sea god Poseidon. His most famous feat was to slay the ferocious Minotaur. King Minos of Crete regularly fed the Minotaur with children from Athens; Theseus volunteered himself to be fed to the Minotaur and, with the help of Minos's daughter Ariadne, killed the Minotaur in the labyrinth (maze) in which he lived.

Yi won a potion of immortality, but Chang E drank it herself and floated to the moon

YI THE ARCHER
The Chinese say that originally there were ten suns, the sons of the emperor of the eastern heavens. The suns took turns lighting the sky. But once, all ten went out to play. Together they were so hot that they began to scorch the Earth, so the emperor sent Yi, the heavenly archer, to teach them a lesson. Yi shot down nine of them. The emperor was so upset that he stripped Yi and his wife, Chang E, of their immortality and banished them from heaven.

Heavenly gates are guarded by two soldiers

Mortals on their way to heaven to become immortals

Perseus holds Medusa's severed head

GREEK GUARDIAN
Perseus was the son of the Greek god Zeus and the maiden Danaë. To save his mother from an unwanted marriage, Perseus agreed to fetch the head of the Gorgon Medusa, whose glance turned the onlooker to stone. Using a bronze shield as a mirror so that he did not have to meet the Gorgon's gaze, Perseus cut off her head. He then used the head to turn his mother's unwelcome suitor to stone.

Kneeling men and women mourn for the dead

Gilgamesh clutches a captured lion cub

Altars full of food

KING GILGAMESH
Gilgamesh was the great hero of ancient Mesopotamia. He was a semidivine king, who fought monsters with his friend Enkidu. When Gilgamesh scorned the love of the goddess Ishtar, she sent a great bull to destroy him, but Gilgamesh and Enkidu slew the bull.

Scenes of the underworld

Medusa lies dead at Perseus's feet

Chinese funeral banner, 2nd century B.C.

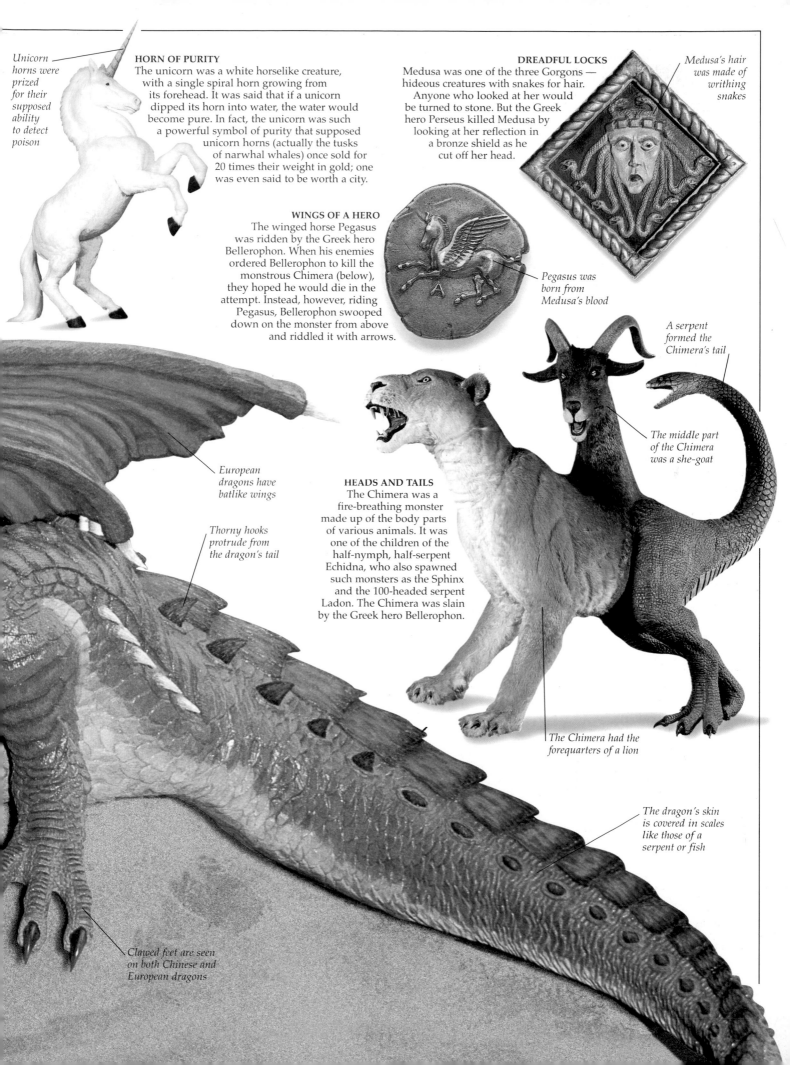

HORN OF PURITY
The unicorn was a white horselike creature, with a single spiral horn growing from its forehead. It was said that if a unicorn dipped its horn into water, the water would become pure. In fact, the unicorn was such a powerful symbol of purity that supposed unicorn horns (actually the tusks of narwhal whales) once sold for 20 times their weight in gold; one was even said to be worth a city.

Unicorn horns were prized for their supposed ability to detect poison

DREADFUL LOCKS
Medusa was one of the three Gorgons — hideous creatures with snakes for hair. Anyone who looked at her would be turned to stone. But the Greek hero Perseus killed Medusa by looking at her reflection in a bronze shield as he cut off her head.

Medusa's hair was made of writhing snakes

WINGS OF A HERO
The winged horse Pegasus was ridden by the Greek hero Bellerophon. When his enemies ordered Bellerophon to kill the monstrous Chimera (below), they hoped he would die in the attempt. Instead, however, riding Pegasus, Bellerophon swooped down on the monster from above and riddled it with arrows.

Pegasus was born from Medusa's blood

A serpent formed the Chimera's tail

The middle part of the Chimera was a she-goat

European dragons have batlike wings

Thorny hooks protrude from the dragon's tail

HEADS AND TAILS
The Chimera was a fire-breathing monster made up of the body parts of various animals. It was one of the children of the half-nymph, half-serpent Echidna, who also spawned such monsters as the Sphinx and the 100-headed serpent Ladon. The Chimera was slain by the Greek hero Bellerophon.

The Chimera had the forequarters of a lion

The dragon's skin is covered in scales like those of a serpent or fish

Clawed feet are seen on both Chinese and European dragons

Painting the story

THERE ARE MANY WAYS OF TELLING stories other than through speech, and many myths are "told" through ritual, dance, or art rather than through narrative storytelling. In the chantways (right) of the Native American Navajo, sand painting, song, prayer, dance, and ritual combine to relive complex myths, which are remembered not for their story content but for their healing spiritual power. The Australian Aboriginal stories of the Dreamtime are recalled not just in words and ceremonies but also through traditional designs painted on the body. The same designs are used in bark paintings and the ground paintings of central Australia, which are very similar to Navajo sand paintings.

BEATING THE DRUM
Across Africa, drums are used to beat out rhythms to accompany reenactment rituals and dances. A drum is thought to have a spirit living in it, which may possess those who dance to its beat. The *bata* drum, used by the Yoruba tribe of West Africa in ceremonies to honor the thunder god Shango, is said to have been made by Shango to frighten his enemies.

The headdress varies in size and design, according to the character

Noble characters paint their faces green

Heroes wear red jackets

STORIES THROUGH DANCE
Kathakali dancers enact stories from the two great epics of India, the Mahabharata and the Ramayana. The essence of both stories is the eternal struggle between good and evil, and dances usually end with the conquering of a demon by a hero.

Wooden snake stick (symbol of lightning)

SNAKE DANCE
Native Americans held rituals to ensure rain and good crops. In the Hopi snake dance, dancers hold live snakes in their mouths. Snake sticks are set up in ceremonial chambers. After the dance, the snakes are released to take the dancers' prayers to the gods.

Beats of the double-sided drum call up new creations

Ankle bracelets

The skirt is made up of many layers of white cotton

RING OF FLAMES
The Hindu god Siva dances the tandava, which represents the creation and destruction of the world. He dances in a circle of flames — one hand cupping the flame of destruction, the other holding the drum of creation. As he dances, Siva tramples the dwarf of ignorance beneath his feet.

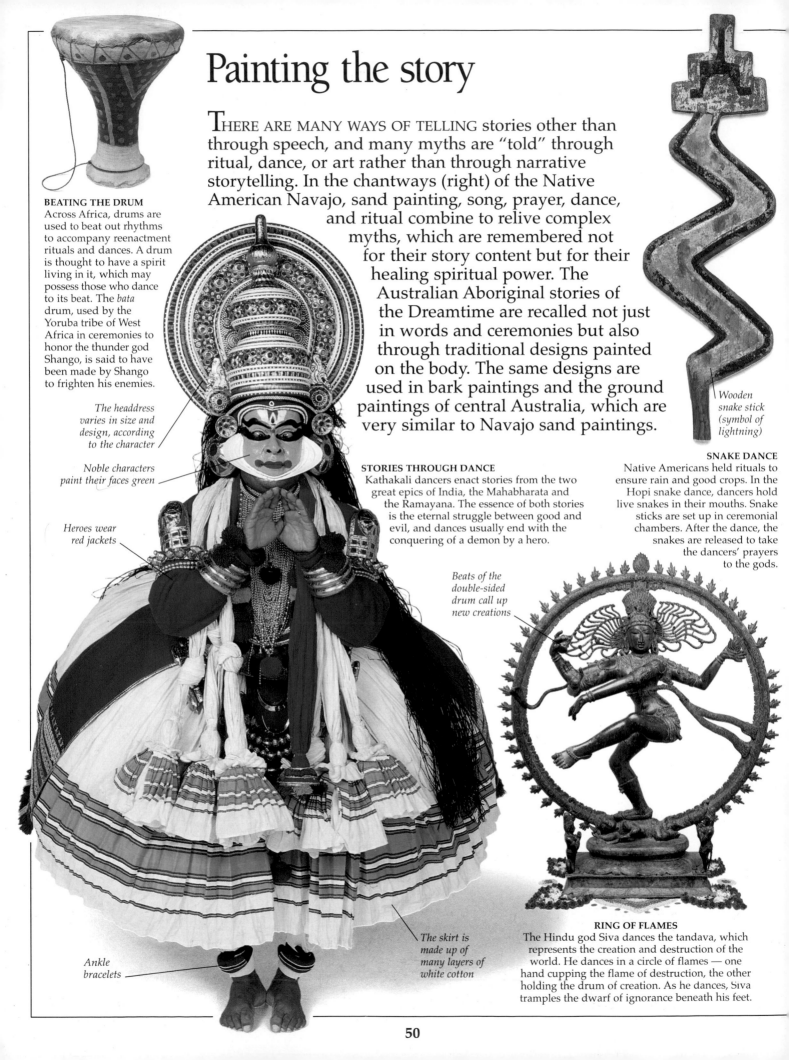

Sacred sandpainting

The sand paintings of the Native American Navajo are temporary altars created and destroyed as part of healing rituals known as chantways. Their Navajo name means "place where the gods come and go." Each painting must be re-created in exactly the same way each time, or the ritual will not work.

Mudstone

Sandstone

Gypsum

Chalk

Brown pigment

Yellow pigment

Red pigment

Charcoal

POWDER PAINTS
Sand painting pigments are gathered by the family sponsoring the ceremony and ground in a mortar and pestle. Pigments include sandstone, mudstone, charcoal from hard oak, cornmeal, powdered flower petals, and plant pollen.

CHANTWAY CEREMONIES
Sand paintings are made by skilled painters under the direction of the singer who is in charge of the ritual. An average sand painting takes six men about four hours to complete. When the painting is finished, the singer sprinkles it with protective pollen and says a prayer; then the ritual begins.

Only men can become qualified sand painters

Pigments are trickled onto the sand through the thumb and forefinger

The Oculate Being has bulging eyes

POWERFUL PICTURES
Sand paintings contain exact depictions of the Navajo "holy people" — supernatural beings whose powers are evoked in the chantway ceremonies. Such sand paintings are sacred and powerful. This nonsacred sand painting, made for commercial sale, shows a typical holy person.

Bracelets and armlets hang from the wrists and elbows

Snake-like tongue

WOVEN STORY
This woven textile from the Paracas people of Peru is full of the spirits and demons of Paracas mythology, including bug-eyed Oculate Beings, shown as heads with no bodies and long tongues snaking out between prominent teeth.

Alpaca wool weaving from southern Peru, 600–200 B.C.

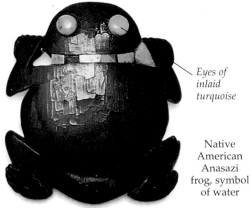

Universal creatures

MANY COMMON THEMES run through world mythology. One theme connects human beings with other animals — we are descended from them, or they are our reincarnated ancestors, or they represent gods or spirits whom we must worship or appease. In many creation myths, such as the stories of the Aboriginal Dreamtime, the first inhabitants of the world are neither animal nor human but a mixture of both. This is true of many "animal" gods, such as the African spider-man Anansi. The Egyptian gods all have one or more animal forms as well as human forms; even in the Judeo-Christian tradition the devil can take the form of a snake.

TURTLE WORLD
Many Native American peoples believe that the Earth is supported on the back of a turtle — a belief that is also found in Hindu mythology. The creator god Brahma took the shape of a turtle to create the world. Vishnu became a turtle to help the gods win the elixir of immortality. In North America and in Africa the turtle is also a trickster figure.

Eyes of inlaid turquoise

Native American Anasazi frog, symbol of water

THE FROG
A West African story telling how Frog brought death into the world is echoed by a Native American myth which says that Frog was so angry with his Maker that he spat poison into the Maker's water, killing him and all his creatures. To the Maori of New Zealand, the frog was a rain god, an association also made by Native Americans. In Egypt Heket was a frog goddess of childbirth and resurrection.

Recurring crocodiles

Because of their fearsome appearance, crocodiles appear in many myths. Often they are threatening creatures — for instance the Basuto tribe of Africa believes that a crocodile can seize a man's shadow and pull him under water. But on the island of Sulawesi, in Indonesia, crocodiles are addressed as "grandfather" because they may be an ancestor. And it is believed that a crocodile will attack a human only when told to do so by the god Poe Mpalaburu.

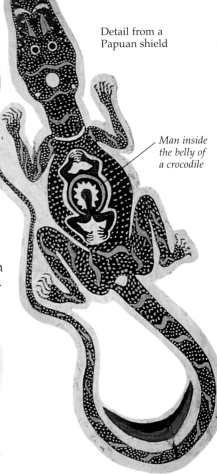

Detail from a Papuan shield

Man inside the belly of a crocodile

FATHER CROCODILE
Papuans believe that crocodiles have magical powers. One myth of the Kiwai Papuans tells how the creator, Ipila, carved the first four humans from wood and gave them sago to eat. But two of them began to eat meat and turned into crocodile-men. The clans descended from them claim the crocodile as their father.

Turquoise mosaic squares

Coral pieces add color to the nose and mouth

Ceremonial snake pendant worn by priests of the Aztec rain god Tlaloc

LIFE-GIVING SERPENT
The snake is probably the most widely revered creature in world mythology. It is often associated with the primal waters from which all life was created. In the Americas, the double-headed serpent is associated with life-giving rain. Australian Aborigines credit the creation of the landscape to the Rainbow Snake, the source of shamanic power. The Rainbow Snake Aido-Hwedo arches over the sky and under the sea in West Africa.

Egyptian
crocodile god
Sobek

Mayan crocodile
incense burner

*The crocodile has
large, snapping jaws
with very sharp teeth*

HEAVENLY MONSTER
In Mayan art there are numerous depictions of
the celestial, or cosmic, monster, a being with a
crocodile's body and two heads, one at the front
and one at the back. The monster is sometimes
shown arching
over the heavens,
its body in the
form of clouds.

Clawed feet

*Golden crocodile
figure made by the
Ashanti people of
West Africa*

*Dry, scaly skin
prevents water
loss in the hot
African sun*

*Back feet
are webbed*

Nile crocodiles
are found on
riverbanks
throughout
tropical Africa

*Powerful,
whiplike tail*

AFRICAN ANCESTORS
Many Africans believe crocodiles
to be reincarnated people. In West
Africa it is said that a person who
kills a crocodile will become one.
And if someone is attacked by a
crocodile, it is believed that the
victim must have harmed the
crocodile during its human life.

RAVENOUS SOBEK
Ancient Egyptians worshipped
crocodiles in the form of the crocodile
god Sobek, who was often depicted with
the head of a crocodile and the body of a
human. Sobek was so hungry that when the
dismembered body of Osiris was thrown into
the Nile, he ate some of it. The other gods
cut out Sobek's tongue for this wicked act.

Death and the underworld

SINCE HUMANITY BEGAN, PEOPLE HAVE told stories to explain what happens after death. The Mayan hero twins Hunahpu and Xbalanque descended to Xibalba, the "place of fright," to rescue their father from One Death, lord of the underworld. The twins survived ordeals in the houses of lances, fire, and jaguars. They then boasted that they had power over death, and to prove it let themselves be killed and ground like flour. When they came back to life, the lords of death were so impressed that they asked to be killed too. But the twins did not revive them, and so the power of death was lessened forever. In his top hat and dark glasses, the Haitian voodoo god Ghede guards the eternal crossroads where the souls of the dead pass their way to the underworld.

The skeleton is commonly used as an image of death

CHINESE JUDGE OF THE DEAD
Yen-lo is the terrifying ruler and judge of the dead in China. First, the souls are weighed: the virtuous are light, the sinful heavy. Then the souls must pass a number of tests and challenges. They are assaulted by demons, attacked by dogs, then allowed one last glimpse of home and family before being given a drink that wipes away all memories. Finally, each soul is reincarnated.

DYING FOR DISOBEDIENCE
The elaborate funeral rites of the Dogon people of West Africa involve dancing and chanting in a secret language. These rituals recount a myth that describes how death entered the world because of the disobedience of young men. Africans do not see death as a final end but believe that the spirits of the dead have power over the living.

Osiris, god of the underworld

Horus, son of Osiris

Skirts are red to represent death

THE AFTERLIFE
The ancient Egyptians believed that their souls would be weighed against the feather of truth, and that they would then be led into the Hall of the Two Truths to face the lord of the dead, Osiris. The virtuous hoped for a new life in the Field of Reeds, a perfected version of Egypt.

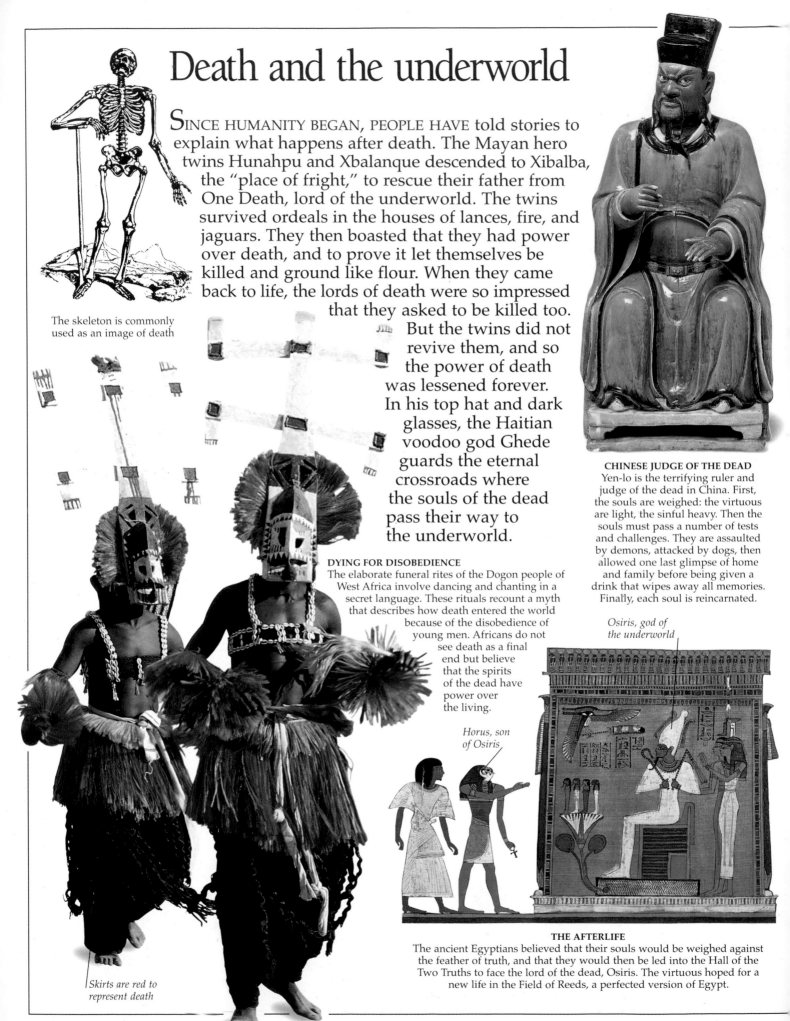

MORTAL A being that will live for a limited time and then die

MUMMIFIED Describes a body that has been turned into a mummy – preserved so that it will not decay

MYTH A story about gods or heroes that often explains how the world came to be as it is or how people should live in it. In everyday speech the word "myth" is sometimes used to mean an untruth.

NEOLITHIC The New Stone Age, which began around the time of the last ice age. Neolithic people used more complex stone tools, built stone structures, and began to make pottery.

NIRVANA In Buddhism and Hinduism, the state of supreme happiness and enlightenment – awareness of the true nature of human existence

NYMPH In Greek mythology, a beautiful young woman who usually has one divine parent. Nereids and oceanids were sea nymphs, naiads were water nymphs, oreads were mountain nymphs, and dryads were tree nymphs.

ORACLE Either a place where the words of a god are revealed or the person through whom a god speaks

PAGAN A person who follows a religion other than Christianity, Judaism, or Islam

PEGASUS A mythical winged horse

PHARAOH The title given to the rulers of ancient Egypt. The word means "great house" and originally referred to the king's palace rather than the king.

PIGMENT The chemicals that give a thing its coloring. In their sacred sandpaintings, Navajos use pigments made from plants and minerals.

PRIMORDIAL Existing at or from the very beginning of creation

PROSPERITY Having good fortune, money, and success

PYRAMID A massive stone structure with a square base and sloping sides. These could be royal tombs, as in Egypt, or sacrificial temples, as in Mesoamerica.

REINCARNATION The belief that a dead person is reborn in another body

An Aztec sacrificial knife

Ritual mask worn by an African shaman

RESURRECTION Rising from the dead or being restored to life

RITE A religious or spiritual ceremony

RITUAL A formalized set of actions and words in which gods are worshipped or asked for help

SACRED Holy or revered

SACRIFICE An offering made to please or placate a god, usually at a cost to the giver. A sacrifice can be a slaughtered animal or even a human being.

SHAMAN A priest or medicine man, whose role is to look after the health and spiritual welfare of the tribe. He does this by carrying out and presiding over special rituals that will influence good or evil spirits.

SHRINE A sacred place dedicated to or associated with a god, spirit, or holy object

SOOTHSAYING Telling fortunes or predicting the future

SORCEROR A wizard or magician who casts spells and has magic powers

SPIRIT A bodiless person or being

SUPERNATURAL Magical or spiritual and beyond the laws of nature

TORII The entrance to a Shinto temple. Usually painted red, it consists of two vertical wooden posts, topped with two horizontal beams, of which the topmost extends beyond the supports.

TOTEM Native American name for a spiritual ancestor. A totem can be a living creature, for example an eagle, or an inanimate thing, such as a river.

TRIBE A group of people who are often related and share the same language and culture

TRICKSTER A person or god who plays tricks or deceives

TSUNAMI A huge sea wave, usually triggered by a volcano or earthquake

UNDERWORLD Mythical region below the Earth where people are said to live after death

UNICORN A mythical horse with a spiral horn on its forehead

VALHALLA In Norse mythology, the great hall of Odin, where dead heroes spend the afterlife, feasting and fighting

VALKYRIE In Norse mythology, one of the female battle spirits who guide heroes to Valhalla

VISION A mystical or religious experience in which a person sees a god or spirit

YANG (*see also* YIN) In Chinese philosophy, one of the two complementary principles. Yang is positive, active, bright, warm, and masculine.

YIN (*see also* YANG) In Chinese philosophy, one of the two complementary principles. Yin is negative, passive, dark, cold, and feminine.

This ornate Viking stone, found on the Swedish island of Gotland, shows a Norse warrior riding into Valhalla

72-page Eyewitness Titles

Other Eyewitness Titles

Introduction

WHAT KIND of people do we want to be? What kind of people do we want our children to be? What kind of moral examples, teachings, choices—personal, community, and political—are we parents, grandparents, and community adults prepared to make at this turn of the century and millennium to make our children strong inside and empowered to seek and help build a more just, compassionate, and less violent society and world?

Over two thousand years ago, a Palestinian Jew named Jesus taught that "Man shall not live by bread alone." His message is in danger of being lost as so many of our children of privilege and poverty chase material idols that fade, and stuff themselves with the cultural junk foods of violence, drugs, and material things that fail to fill the deeper hunger for community and purpose all humans share.

The twentieth century was characterized by stunning scientific and technological progress. We split the atom, pierced space, walked on the moon, landed on Mars, and broke the genetic code. Instant communication led to an information explosion and daily money trading in the trillions. We witnessed astonishing increases in wealth resulting from a tiny microchip. We can fly through the air faster than the speed of sound and cruise the seas quicker than the creatures inhabiting them. We created the capacity to feed the world's population and to prevent the poverty that afflicts the majority of humankind. But something is missing. Our scientific and military progress have not been accompanied by comparable moral progress.

Every child today is infected by our violence-saturated culture and excessive consumerism. Buying is equated with happiness. Possessing things is equated with success. Children are marketed sex, alcohol, tobacco, and violence as the way to be accepted.

I believe the prophets, the Gospels, the Koran, other great faiths, history, moral decency, and common sense beckon us to examine anew as individuals and as a people what we are to live by and teach our children. Parents, grandparents, teachers, preachers, neighbors, people of conscience, and people of faith must lift a strong counter voice to the corrupting messages of our culture and teach our children that they can make a difference.

Making a difference is the organizing framework for this book. I believe each of us is put on this earth for a purpose and with the duty to make this world a better place. My parents and Black community elders taught, by word and deed, that service is the rent each of us pays for living and that the only thing that lasts is what is shared with others. They passed down the habit of service and created opportunities for children to serve at very young ages. They also taught that service and charity are not enough—that we have to raise our voices for justice and freedom also. If we don't like the way the world is, we can do our part to change it. Success is never guaranteed, but contributing to the struggle is a responsibility and a privilege.

How can we make a difference? In this book, I have selected twelve essential ways in which children can make a difference in their lives and in the lives of those around them. I have chosen quotes, stories, and poems from cultures around the world to illustrate these twelve values and to inspire the children and parents who read them together.

The principles outlined in this book are:

1. I can make a difference by loving myself and others as God loves us and treating others respectfully and fairly.
2. I can make a difference by being courageous.
3. I can make a difference by aiming high and holding on to my ideals.
4. I can make a difference by caring and serving.
5. I can make a difference by being honest and telling the truth.

6. I can make a difference by persevering and not giving up.

7. I can make a difference by being determined and resourceful.

8. I can make a difference by being grateful for the gift and wonders of life.

9. I can make a difference by working together with others.

10. I can make a difference by being compassionate and kind.

11. I can make a difference by being nonviolent and working for peace.

12. I can make a difference by being faithful and struggling for what I believe.

I hope this book will inspire and empower children through the stories and wisdom of the many cultures and peoples with whom our children must share a world. All our children need to know that goodness and wisdom come in all colors and countries and genders and sizes and do not belong to any single person or group or nation. I also hope this book will help build children strong on the inside, with spiritual anchors to meet challenges with resiliency, knowing always what Ralph Waldo Emerson said: "What lies behind us and what lies before us are tiny matters compared to what lies within us."

We can all make a difference.

1.

I can make a difference

by loving myself and others as

God loves us and treating

others respectfully and fairly.

PEOPLE OF different religions and beliefs disagree on many things. But all major religions agree on treating your neighbor—who is all other human beings—as you would like to be treated.

Every major religion teaches us to love each other as ourselves.

Christianity—All things whatsoever you would that others should do to you, do you even so to them.

Judaism—Thou shalt love thy neighbor as thyself.

Islam—No one of you is a believer until he loves for his brother what he loves for himself.

Hinduism—Good people proceed while considering what is best for others is best for themselves.

Zoroastrianism—Whatever is disagreeable to yourself do not do to others.

Buddhism—Hurt not others with that which pains yourself.

Confucianism—What you do not want done to yourself do not do unto others.

Taoism—Regard your neighbor's gain as your own gain, and regard your neighbor's loss as your own loss.

I have a dream that my four little children will one day live in a nation where they will not be judged by the color of their skin but by the content of their character.

—The Rev. Dr. Martin Luther King, Jr.

Dear Dr. King,

   We could sure use your help nowadays. Not only has segregation between Blacks and Whites started again, but now some people are rude in helping people of their own color. . . . Many of the handicapped and disabled children only have each other, because people think they have something that others can catch and it caused them to become that way. Children in schools pick their friends, and many of the "strange ones," as they would put it, don't get picked.

—Kimberly, age 11

Each second we live in a new and unique moment of the universe, a moment that never was before and will never be again. And what do we teach our children in school? We teach them that two and two make four, and that Paris is the capital of France. When will we also teach them what they are? We should say to each of them: Do you know what you are? You are a marvel. You are unique. In all of the world there is no other child exactly like you. In the millions of years that have passed there has never been another child like you. And look at your body—what a wonder it is! your legs, your arms, your cunning fingers, the way you move! You may become a Shakespeare, a Michelangelo, a Beethoven. You have the capacity for anything. Yes, you are a marvel. And when you grow up, can you then harm another who is, like you, a marvel? You must cherish one another. You must work—we all must work—to make this world worthy of its children.

—*Pablo Casals*

A Love Poem to Every Special Child

BLACK AND BROWN girl dark of hue with kinky or curly hair
White child with straight hair and freckles too
God painted your skin and curled and straightened your hair just for you.
God is love and you are God's beloved.
Black, Brown, Yellow, Red, and White child created to look just like you,
    God rejoices and is glad in you.
God is love and you are God's beloved.
Special child who sees and discerns without the eyes and ears and speech the rest
    of us need
who navigates without the legs ordinary people require and manages without
    the hands on which other mortals depend.
God is love and you are God's beloved.
Weary child of the night and castaway of the streets afraid and abused
in need of safe haven and home to rest and to nest.
God is love and you are God's beloved.
Child of slow mind, innocent of worldly wiles and the will to harm others, freed
    of devious thoughts.
God is love and you are God's beloved.
Child of poverty unburdened by the chains of things and greed which imprison
    the haves too muches.
God came in your disguise to save us all.
God is love and you are God's beloved.

—*Marian Wright Edelman*

Just Me

Nobody sees what I can see,
For back of my eyes there is only me.
And nobody knows how my thoughts begin,
For there's only myself inside my skin.
Isn't it strange how everyone owns
Just enough skin to cover his bones?
My father's would be too big to fit—
I'd be all wrinkled inside of it.
And my baby brother's is much too small—
It just wouldn't cover me up at all.
But I feel just right in the skin I wear,
And there's nobody like me anywhere.

—*Margaret Hillert*

2.

I can make a difference

by being courageous.

You gain strength, courage, and confidence by every
experience in which you really stop to look fear in the face. . . .
You must do the thing you think you cannot do.

—*Eleanor Roosevelt*

Life Doesn't Frighten Me

SHADOWS ON the wall
Noises down the hall
Life doesn't frighten me at all
Bad dogs barking loud
Big ghosts in a cloud
Life doesn't frighten me at all.

Mean old Mother Goose
Lions on the loose
They don't frighten me at all
Dragons breathing flame
On my counterpane
That doesn't frighten me at all.

I go boo
Make them shoo
I make fun
Why they run
I won't cry
So they fly
I just smile
They go wild
Life doesn't frighten me at all.

Tough guys in a fight
All alone at night
Life doesn't frighten me at all.

Panthers in the park
Strangers in the dark
No, they don't frighten me at all.

That new classroom where
Boys all pull my hair
(Kissy little girls
With their hair in curls)
They don't frighten me at all.

Don't show me frogs and snakes
And listen for my scream,
If I'm afraid at all
It's only in my dreams.

I've got a magic charm
That I keep up my sleeve,
I can walk the ocean floor
And never have to breathe.

Life doesn't frighten me at all
Not at all
Not at all.
Life doesn't frighten me at all.

—*Maya Angelou*

Li Chi and the Serpent

ONCE, IN ANCIENT days, in the Kingdom of Yueh, a terrible serpent came to live in the Yung Mountains. There it coiled around the rocks and sent dreadful dream messages to everyone—*I will destroy the land and all the people if I am not given maidens to eat.*

Oh, the wailing and moaning that followed the hearing of this threat. What could the people possibly do?

"We can't let our maidens be eaten!" they cried.

So the people sent for brave heroes to kill the serpent for them. The heroes swaggered boldly up to the mountain peak. But when they saw the serpent, with its terrible fangs and claws, every one of those heroes ran away.

"Enough delay!" the serpent roared at the people. "I will destroy you all if I am not given maidens to eat, and quickly!"

"What can we do now?" the people wailed. "We have no heroes left! We will surely have to give the serpent the maidens it wishes."

And so, a hunt for maidens began. Word of this dreadful search reached the family of a poor farmer, Li Tan. Li Tan had once been a soldier, but that had been long ago. Now he was a father with six daughters, and his old sword hung on the wall, slowly rusting.

When Li Tan and his daughters heard about the serpent, they began to weep at the thought that one of them might well be chosen to be eaten.

Only the youngest of the six daughters, Li Chi, did not waste time weeping. "Why should I cry about something that might never happen?" she told her father. "And I refuse to let myself be frightened of a creature that I have never seen!"

Instead, Li Chi began to wonder just how such a monster might be stopped. And an idea came to her.

"Let me be chosen," she told her father.

"No!" he cried in horror.

"Yes," she insisted. "Only be sure the officials who come for me give you a nice ransom in exchange for me. That way, no matter what happens, my sisters will have some money on which to live. Oh, Father, don't worry. I have no intention of letting myself be eaten. And I have no intention of letting any other girls be eaten either!"

The officials came for her very soon. "I will come with you," Li Chi said humbly. "But first, let me take a memory of home with me."

So she took her father's rusty sword, the farm's snake-hunting dog, and a sack of sweet rice with her. She let the officials lead her up to the mountain peak. There, Li Chi seated herself comfortably and began rolling the sweet rice into tasty treats. These she placed at the entrance of the serpent's cave. Then she hid in the shadows to wait, holding the snake-hunting dog so that he would not whine or bark.

The serpent smelled the sweet rice and came out of the cave. Oh, but he was terrible to see with teeth sharp as spears and eyes bright and fierce as flames. Hiding in the shadows, Li Chi bit her lip to keep from crying out in fear.

The serpent paused, looking down at the sweet rice. *What is this? These strange objects smell interesting, indeed!* After a wary look around, he lowered his head and began to eat.

"Now!" Li Chi whispered to the dog, and let him loose. The serpent smelled just like a snake to the dog, and he bit the monster with all his might. The serpent roared in surprise and whirled toward the dog—and as he did, he left his long neck exposed. Li Chi raised her father's sword and struck down with all her strength, cutting that serpent's head right off.

"You will never eat another maiden," Li Chi said, and went home.

Word of Li Chi's feat reached the King of Yueh. He went to visit her father's farm. He liked what he saw of Li Chi so much—and she liked what she saw of him, too—that he made her his queen. She and all her family lived happily at court from then on.

And no other monsters ever troubled the Kingdom of Yueh again.

—A tale from China

3.

I can make a difference

by aiming high and

holding on to my ideals.

No pessimist ever discovered the secret of the stars, or sailed to an uncharted land, or opened a new doorway for the human spirit.

—*Helen Keller*

If you have built castles in the air, your work need not be lost; that is where they should be. Now put the foundations under them.

—*Henry David Thoreau*

It must be borne in mind that the tragedy of life doesn't lie in not reaching your goal. The tragedy lies in having no goal to reach. It isn't a calamity to die with dreams unfulfilled, but it is a calamity not to dream.
It is not a disaster to be unable to capture your ideal, but it is a disaster to have no ideal to capture. It is not a disgrace not to reach the stars, but it is a disgrace to have no stars to reach for. Not failure, but low aim is sin.

—*Dr. Benjamin E. Mays*

If You Think You Are Beaten

IF YOU THINK you are beaten, you are;
If you think that you dare not, you don't;
If you'd like to win, but you think you can't,
It's almost a cinch that you won't.

If you think you'll lose, you've lost;
For out in the world you'll find
Success begins with a person's will,
It's all in the state of mind.

Full many a race is lost
Ere even a step is run,
And many a coward falls
Ere even his work's begun.

—*Anonymous*

Listen to the Mustn'ts

Listen to the MUSTN'TS, child,
Listen to the DON'TS
Listen to the SHOULDN'TS
The IMPOSSIBLES, the WON'TS
Listen to the NEVER HAVES
Then listen close to me—
Anything can happen, child,
ANYTHING can be.

—*Shel Silverstein*

Speech to the Young
Speech to the Progress-Toward

For Nora Brooks Blakely
For Henry Blakely III

SAY TO them,
say to the down-keepers,
the sun-slappers,
the self-foilers,
The harmony-hushers,
"Even if you are not ready for day
it cannot always be night."
You will be right.
For that is the hard home-run.

And remember:
live not for Battles Won.
Live not for The-End-of-the-Song.
Live for the along.

—*Gwendolyn Brooks*

Sojourner Truth

4.

I can make a difference

by caring and serving.

How lovely to think that no one need wait a moment,
we can start now, start slowly changing the world!
—*Anne Frank*

Facing a heckler once who told her he did not care for her antislavery talk
any more than he would for the bite of a flea, Sojourner Truth retorted,
"Perhaps not, but Lord willing, I'll keep you scratching."

A Prayer for Each of Us to Serve

LORD, I cannot preach like Martin Luther King, Jr.
or turn a poetic phrase like Maya Angelou
but I care and am willing to serve.

I do not have Fred Shuttlesworth's and
Harriet Tubman's courage
or Eleanor and Franklin Roosevelt's political skills
but I care and am willing to serve.

I cannot sing like Fannie Lou Hamer
or organize like Ella Baker and Bayard Rustin
but I care and am willing to serve.

I am not holy like Archbishop Tutu,
forgiving like Mandela, or disciplined like Gandhi
but I care and am willing to serve.

I am not brilliant like Dr. Du Bois or
Elizabeth Cady Stanton,
or as eloquent as Sojourner Truth and
Booker T. Washington
but I care and am willing to serve.

I have not Mother Teresa's saintliness,
Dorothy Day's love or
Cesar Chavez's gentle tough spirit
but I care and am willing to serve.

God, it is not as easy as the 60s
to frame an issue and forge a solution
but I care and am willing to serve.

My mind and body are not so swift as in youth
and my energy comes in spurts
but I care and am willing to serve.

I'm so young
nobody will listen
I'm not sure what to say or do
but I care and am willing to serve.

I can't see or hear well
speak good English, stutter sometimes
and get real scared standing up before others
but I care and am willing to serve.

Use me as Thou will to save Thy children today and tomorrow
and to build a nation and world where no
child is left behind and everyone feels welcome.

—*Marian Wright Edelman*

Holding Up the Sky

ONE DAY an elephant saw a hummingbird lying
on its back with its tiny feet up in the air. "What
are you doing?" asked the elephant.

The hummingbird replied,
"I heard that the sky might fall today,
and so I am ready to help hold it up,
should it fall."

The elephant laughed cruelly.
"Do you really think," he said,
"that those tiny feet could help hold up the sky?"

The hummingbird kept his feet up in the air,
intent on his purpose, as he replied,
"Not alone. But each must do what he can.
And this is what I can do."

—*A tale from China*

WHAT ACTIONS are
most excellent?

To gladden the heart
of a human being.
To feed the hungry.
To help the afflicted.
To lighten the sorrow
of the sorrowful.
To remove the wrongs
of the injured.
That person is the
most beloved of God
who does most good
to God's creatures.

—*The Prophet Muhammed*

The Generous Physician

GENEROUS EVEN IN THOUGHT WAS ABBA UMANA,
WHO DISARMED CRITICISM BY NOT MAKING USE OF IT.

ABBA UMANA was a physician who had attained great celebrity, so that he was known as Father, or Chief, of the Skillful. His fame was further amplified by tales of his generosity.

For instance, he was most considerate of a patient's pride. He would not name a fee, lest it be more than the sick person could afford. He had a box set up in a private corner of his house, where those who came to him for advice and treatment would deposit whatever they could pay. If without means, they need not be put to shame, while the rich could give genuine proof of their gratitude.

It worked out very well for Abba Umana. He was able to live comfortably; and the report of his magnanimity spread beyond his own land.

It spread to faraway Babylonia, where Abbayé was head of the Talmudic academy. Two of his pupils were sick and seemed to make no progress under the treatment of neighboring physicians. Abbayé sent for them. "You shall go, my sons," he said, "to Abba Umana. Money for the journey will be provided, and for your lodging

30

in the town until, God willing, you be cured. In the meantime, satisfy my curiosity about that saintly man. See if he is really as generous and good as they say."

The students set out. When they came to Abba Umana, he diagnosed their ailment and said: "You must come to me every day for treatment. Meanwhile, as students journeying from so far away, you shouldn't be allowed to waste your money paying for lodgings. Stay in my house and be my guests until you recover. You will be welcome. There's nothing I like better than hearing about travel and foreign lands and different customs."

As for putting money in the box, Abba Umana would not hear of it. "I should pay *you*," he said, "for the pleasure of your company!"

The students spent several days in great comfort at Abba Umana's house. They joined him at meals, while he listened delightedly to their college gossip and drew them out about their teachers and the government of the community. They shared an excellent room and enjoyed the sights of the city.

In short they felt an increasing unwillingness to make trial of their kind host's generosity. They already knew him as the finest person they had ever met. Still, to obey the request of the fatherly Abbayé, they planned to put their doctor to a test.

When he told them they were cured but asked them to remain with him a day or two longer, they thanked him and assented.

Before dawn on the following morning, without a word or message of farewell, they stole out of the house, taking with them the rich silken tapestry that had covered their bed. They took their stand in the marketplace at a spot where they knew Abba Umana must pass in his daily routine, and offered the coverlet for sale.

As the physician came up to them, they shamelessly displayed it and asked him what he would pay for it. "Seven gold pieces," said

Abba Umana amiably. "At least, that is what I paid for a coverlet very much like it." And to their amazement, he took that sum from his purse and gave it to them.

"But do you not see," exclaimed one of the students, not closing his hand on the gold, "that this is your own property?"

"We stole it from your house," cried the other youth. "Aren't you going to call us thieves—and—and ingrates?"

Abba Umana laughed indulgently. "You must have a good reason for what you are doing. From what I have seen of you, you cannot be thieves. It may be you have a righteous purpose in mind. Perhaps you want to raise money for a special good deed, such, for instance, as buying a Jewish slave or captive in order to release him, and are merely ashamed to say so."

"Our only purpose," they told him, "was to put your generosity and faith in humankind to the test. And we're content. All the praise that has been given you is well deserved!"

"What flattery is this that you pour into an old man's ears!" the physician rejoined. He would not accept the coverlet. "I have enough of such things," he said. "Besides, in my mind I knew you had good intentions and I already devoted it to a charitable purpose. Consequently, it is no longer mine."

"But we have no place for it," the students insisted. "It is far too handsome for our use."

"Sell it, then, and divide the money among the poor." Abba Umana sighed. "Look about you! There are far too many who need it!"

That was the satisfying story they brought back to Abbayé.

—A traditional Jewish tale

If I can stop one Heart from breaking
I shall not live in vain
If I can ease one Life the Aching
Or cool one Pain

Or help one fainting Robin
Unto his Nest again
I shall not live in Vain.

—*Emily Dickinson*

5.

I can make a difference

by being honest

and telling the truth.

Once to every man and nation comes the moment to decide,
In the strife of Truth with Falsehood, for the good or evil side.

—*James Russell Lowell*

Fire, Water, Truth, and Falsehood

Long ago, Fire, Water, Truth, and Falsehood lived together in one large house. They were considerate of one another, but tried to stay out of one another's way. Truth and Falsehood sat as far apart as they could, and Fire stayed out of Water's way.

One day the four housemates went hunting together. They found a herd of cattle and began driving them home. Truth spoke up and said, "Let us divide the cattle equally among us, for that is the only fair way." No one disagreed.

But as they walked, Falsehood decided that it would be better to have more than an even share of the cattle, and so Falsehood went over to Water and said, "You are more powerful than Fire. Destroy Fire, and there will be more cattle for all of us."

Water flowed over to Fire, who soon went out in a steaming burst of smoke. Now there were only three.

Falsehood whispered to Truth, "Look how Water has destroyed Fire. Let's leave Water and go high into the mountains so our cattle can graze."

Higher and higher they climbed, and since water cannot flow upward, it could not follow. Water washed down the slope, as it does to this day.

When Truth and Falsehood reached the mountaintop, Falsehood turned on Truth and said, "I am more powerful than you! You are now my servant. I am your master. All the cattle belong to me!"

But Truth would not agree. "I will never be your servant!" he cried.

They fought bitterly until finally they decided to bring their argument to Wind. Wind would decide who the master was. But Wind didn't know. Wind blew all over the world, asking people whether Truth or Falsehood was more powerful. Some people said, "A single word of Falsehood can destroy Truth." Others said, "Like a small candle in the dark, one word of Truth can change everything."

Wind listened carefully to what everyone had to say and returned with an answer. Wind said, "I see now that Falsehood is very powerful. But it can only rule where Truth has stopped struggling to be heard."

—An Ethiopian tale from northeast Africa

Feathers

A sharp-tongued woman was accused
   of starting a rumor. When she
   was brought before the village
   rabbi, she said, "I was only
   joking. My words were spread by
   others, and so I am not to blame."
But the victim demanded justice,
   saying, "Your words soiled my
   good name!"
"I'll take back what I said," replied
   the sharp-tongued woman, "and
   that will take away my guilt."
   When the rabbi heard this, he knew
   that this woman truly did not
   understand her crime.
And so he said to the woman, "Your
   words will not be excused until you
   have done the following. Bring my
   feather pillow to the market square.
   Cut it and let the feathers fly
   through the air. Then collect every
   one of the feathers from the pillow
   and bring them all back to me.
   When you have done this, you will
   be absolved of your crime."

The woman agreed, but thought to herself, The old rabbi has finally gone mad!

She did as he asked, and cut the pillow. Feathers blew far and wide over the square and beyond. The wind carried them here and there, up into trees and under merchants' carts. She tried to catch them, but after much effort it was clear to her that she would never find them all.

She returned to the rabbi with only a few feathers in her hand. Facing the rabbi, she said, "I could not take back the feathers any more than I could take back my words. From now on I will be careful not to say anything that would harm another, for there is no way to control the flight of words, any more than I could control the flight of these feathers." From that day, the woman spoke kindly of all she met.

—A Hasidic tale from Eastern Europe

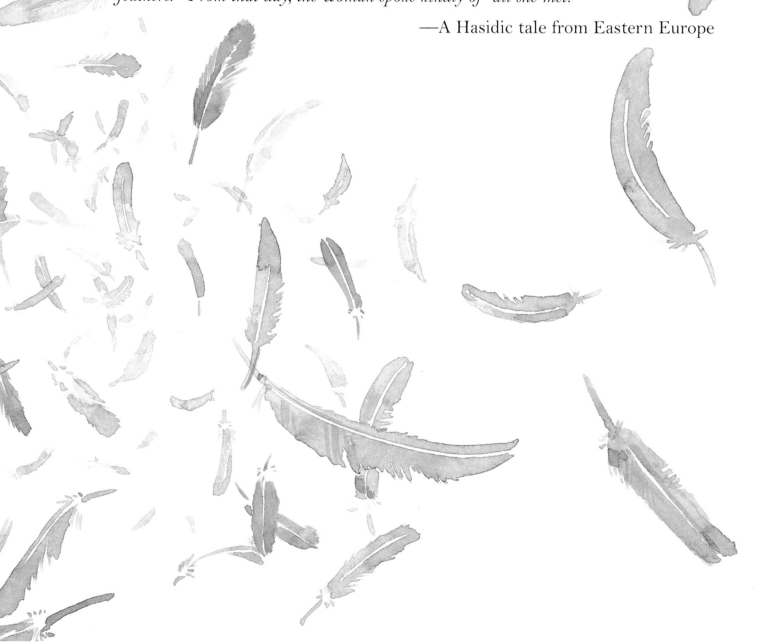

6.

I can make a difference

by persevering and not giving up.

"I think I can—I think I can—I think I can—I think I can—I think I can—I think I can—I think I can—I think I can—I think I can."

—*Watty Piper,* THE LITTLE ENGINE THAT COULD

Mother to Son

WELL, SON, I'll tell you,
Life for me ain't been no crystal stair.
It's had tacks in it,
And splinters,
And boards torn up,
And places with no carpet on the floor—
Bare.
But all the time
I'se been a-climbin' on,
And reachin' landin's,
And turnin' corners,
And sometimes goin' in the dark
Where there ain't been no light.
So, boy, don't you turn back.
Don't you set down on the steps
'Cause you finds it's kinder hard.
Don't you fall now—
For I'se still goin', honey,
I'se still climbin',
And life for me ain't been no crystal stair.

—*Langston Hughes*

The Lion's Whiskers

BIZUNESH, A woman of the Ethiopian highlands, married Gudina, a man of the lowlands. Gudina's first wife had died of a fever, and he had an eight-year-old son whose name was Segab. When Bizunesh went to the house of Gudina, she quickly saw that Segab was a very sad boy because he missed his mother so much.

In only a short time Bizunesh grew to love Segab as if he were her own son, and she tried to be a good mother. She mended all of Segab's clothes and bought him new shoes. She asked him what foods he liked best, and she always saved the choicest pieces of meat from the *wat* for Segab. But Segab did not thank her. He would not even look at her or talk to her.

Bizunesh and Segab were often alone together because Gudina was a merchant who traveled with mule caravans to distant places. Bizunesh worried that Segab would be lonely and tried especially hard to please him when his father was away. "I have always wanted a son," Bizunesh told Segab. "Now God has given me one. I love you very much." Often she tried to kiss him.

But always Segab would turn away from her, and once he shouted, "You are not my mother. I do not love you."

One day Segab ran away from the house and hid in the town market until his father came and found him. When Segab returned home, Bizunesh tried to take him in her arms, but he pulled away from her. He would not touch the bowl of delicious soup she had saved for him. Bizunesh cried all that night.

In the morning Bizunesh went to the hut of a famous wise man. She told the wise man about her new stepson who refused to love her, no matter how hard she tried to please him.

"You must make me a magic love powder," Bizunesh told the old man. "I will put it in Segab's food, and then he will love me."

The wise man was silent for several minutes. "I can do what you ask," he said at last. "But to make such a powder, I must have three whiskers from the ferocious lion who lives in the black-rock desert across the river. Bring the whiskers to me, and I will make the powder for you."

Bizunesh could hardly believe her ears. "How can I get the lion's whiskers?" she asked. "He will surely kill me."

"I cannot tell you how to get the whiskers," the wise man said to Bizunesh. "That is for you to decide. But I must have them before I can make the love powder."

Bizunesh walked sadly from the wise man's hut. She did not sleep a wink that night, but in the morning her mind was made up. Nothing was as important to her as winning Segab's love. She had to try to get three whiskers from the lion even if he ate her. Only then would the wise man make the magic love powder for her.

That very day Bizunesh carried a large piece of raw meat to the black-rock desert. At last she saw the lion standing on a large rock, watching her from a great distance. When the lion jumped from the rock and loped toward her, Bizunesh was terrified. She threw the meat on the ground and ran. Only when she reached the river did she stop and look back. She saw the lion standing over the meat she had dropped. She heard him roar before he began to eat.

Two days later Bizunesh went again to the black-rock desert with a big piece of meat. She saw the lion watching her from the same rock. This time she walked closer to him before the lion jumped down and started toward her. Bizunesh stood still for a moment and watched the lion approach. Then her fear overcame her, and she threw the meat down and ran. When she looked back, she saw the lion eating.

On the following day Bizunesh walked even closer to the lion. This time she placed the meat on the ground and walked slowly away. Before she had gone far, she stopped and watched as the lion came and ate the meat.

Day after day Bizunesh came closer. Finally, she left the meat only a few hundred feet from the lion. The great beast growled, but Bizunesh did not think it sounded like an angry growl. She moved only a few steps away before she stopped and watched the lion eat. The next day Bizunesh left the meat fifty feet from the lion and stayed while he came and ate.

Then a few days later Bizunesh walked right up to the lion and handed him the meat. Her heart pounded with fear, but her love for Segab was so great that she did not run.

She watched the lion's great jaws fly open! Crash shut! She heard the sound of his teeth tearing through the meat. After a moment she reached out with a very sharp knife and cut three whiskers from the lion's muzzle. The lion was so busy eating that he did not even notice.

Bizunesh ran all the way to the wise man's hut. She was out of breath, but she was still able to shout, "I have the lion's whiskers!" She waved them in front of the old wise man. "Now make me the love powder, and Segab will surely love me."

The wise man took the lion's whiskers. He looked at them and then handed them back to Bizunesh. "You do not need a love powder," he told her. "You learned how to approach the lion—slowly. Do the same with Segab, and he will learn to love you."

—A tale from Ethiopia

7.

I can make a difference

by being determined and resourceful.

You must not expect anything from others. It's you, of yourself, of whom you must ask a lot. Only from oneself has one the right to ask everything and anything. This way it's up to you—your own choices—what you get from others remains a present, a gift!

—*Albert Schweitzer*

The Crow and the Pitcher

ONE HOT summer day, a crow was thirsty, so thirsty, in fact, that he felt he would die if he didn't have a cool drink of water. He came upon a tall pitcher, half full of water. The crow perched on the rim and leaned deep into the pitcher, but his beak was not long enough to reach the water. The crow was thirstier than ever now, with cool water so close and yet just out of reach. The crow thought for a moment and sprang into action.

Beneath the windowsill where the pitcher stood was a pile of pebbles. The crow flew down and picked up as many as he could carry. He dropped the pebbles into the pitcher. He repeated this several times, and every time he did, the level of the water rose just a little bit. After many trips, the water nearly reached the top. The crow was then able to drink his fill.

Where there's a will, there's a way.

—Aesop

Necessity

ONCE THERE was a farmer who was blessed with all a farmer could wish for: fine, fertile lands, happy, healthy animals, a comfortable home, and a handsome son, Petr. Petr was a good-natured young man and as loving a son as ever a father could wish for. But because everything went so well on the farm, he knew nothing at all of hardship and want.

His father worried about that. "Petr has never experienced even the slightest bit of ill luck. I don't even know if he could be clever enough to fend for himself if something went wrong! No, no, this will never do. I must find a way to test my boy and see if he can, indeed, overcome some hardship," he said to himself.

From that day on, the farmer gave Petr all the difficult jobs to do, all the tasks that might possibly go wrong. But nothing went wrong!

"This will never do," the farmer mused. "I must find some way to test Petr."

He thought about it and thought about it. Then, late one night, the farmer woke with a laugh. "Ha! I have it! I know exactly how I'll test my Petr."

So the next morning he called his son to him and said, "Petr, I wish you to go on an errand for me."

"Of course, Father. What is it you need?" the son replied.

"I wish you to go into the forest and look for necessity."

Petr frowned. He assumed his father meant for him to go and find a person. But Necessity! That was an odd name for anyone to bear. "And where will I find Mr. Necessity?"

"Don't worry, my boy. If you don't find necessity, necessity will surely find you and teach you a wise lesson. But I don't want you to come home before that happens. Do you understand? You are not to come home until you have found necessity or necessity has found you."

Now Petr was more confused than before. Was the mysterious Necessity a friend of his father's?

Whoever he was, he must be a clever fellow indeed, if he could find someone in that vast forest! "Very well, Father," Petr said reluctantly. "Let me take a horse and—"

"No, no," his father interrupted. "We need all the horses today."

"Then I shall take a sturdy oxcart and—"

"No, no, we shall need all the sturdy oxcarts as well. Here is what you may take."

He led the boy to the most rickety, most worn-out oxcart on the whole farm. "This?" Petr asked. "B-but it will surely fall apart the moment I enter the forest."

"Don't worry," his father said with a smile. "If it does fall apart, necessity will help you fix it."

And so a truly puzzled Petr drove his two oxen off into the forest, the rickety old cart rocking and creaking beneath him. He drove far and long into the forest,

till the tall trees nearly shut out the light with their leaves and he could barely see his way. And all the time he rode, Petr called out: "Mr. Necessity? Mr. Necessity? Can you hear me? Please, Mr. Necessity, I'm looking for you!"

But no one answered. The day wore on, and the night came near, and Petr looked around uneasily. The forest was a very wild place, full of wolves and bears that might want to eat a team of oxen. Or even a boy!

"Mr. Necessity! Please!"

Just then, the oxcart struck a rock and tilted sideways so suddenly that Petr was thrown to the ground. As he picked himself up, the boy groaned.

"Look at this cart. One of the axles has snapped right in half, and there's the wheel, rolled off by itself." Petr glanced around with a shiver. He was alone, all alone in the middle of the wild forest. *And there isn't a glimpse of Mr. Necessity. Now what am I going to do?* the boy wondered to himself.

He sat down on a rock, with his head in his hands, until the oxen, who had been peacefully nibbling on leaves, straightened up with a snort. Petr straightened, too. What was that? Had he heard wolves howling?

"I can't stay here and wait for Mr. Necessity. Father was wrong; he's nowhere

around. I can't walk all the way home, not with the night almost here. So I'll just have to fix the cart myself. But how?"

Petr walked around the cart. The wheels looked all right, but the axle was definitely broken.

"There are many stray branches lying around. I wonder . . . ," Petr thought aloud. He used his belt knife to whittle off a good, straight branch that looked to be the right size.

"Now, how do I hoist the cart up so that I can get the broken axle off and the new one on?" He paused and then said, "I think I know."

Petr took another branch, a strong, springy one. He balanced it on a rock, slipped one end of the branch under the cart, and stood on the other end. Sure enough, the branch acted as a lever, and the cart bed came up off the ground. Petr braced the branch with another rock, so the cart wouldn't fall on him, and set about pulling off the broken axle and slipping in the new one. He fixed both wheels firmly onto the new axle, then let the cart settle back to the ground.

"It worked! The new axle is holding!"

Petr jumped back onto the cart and picked up the reins. "Come, my oxen. Let's go home!"

Meanwhile, Petr's father was pacing back and forth, forth and back. Had he done the right thing, sending his boy off into the forest? Here it was, nearly night, and there wasn't a sign of the boy.

Ah, but here he comes! Here comes Petr now! The father looked at the newly repaired cart and beamed. "My boy, my clever, clever boy, you did find necessity!"

Petr frowned. "I did no such thing. I saw no one in the forest at all, most certainly not any Mr. Necessity. And he didn't teach me a thing! All I learned was that if something needs to be done, you cannot just wait around for someone else to do it. You have to help yourself."

The farmer laughed. "My dear boy, I never meant for you to find a *man* named Necessity! I just wanted to be sure you could solve problems by yourself. And now I can be proud because necessity has taught you a fine lesson after all."

—A tale from Romania

Albert Schweitzer

8.

I can make a difference

by being grateful for the gift

and wonders of life.

Just to be is a blessing. Just to live is holy.

—Rabbi Abraham Joshua Heschel

The greatest thing is to give thanks for everything.
He who has learned this knows what it means to live.
He has penetrated the whole mystery of life:
giving thanks for everything.

—Albert Schweitzer

From *Leaves of Grass*

. . . I KNOW NOTHING else but miracles,

Whether I walk the streets of Manhattan,

Or dart my sight over the roofs of houses toward the sky,

Or wade with naked feet along the beach just in the edge of the water,

Or stand under trees in the woods,

Or talk by day with any one I love, or sleep in bed at night with anyone I love,

Or sit at table at dinner with the rest,

Or look at strangers opposite me riding in the car,

Or watch honey-bees busy around the hive of a summer forenoon,

Or animals feeding in the fields,

Or birds, or the wonderfulness of insects in the air,

Or the exquisite delicate thin curve of the new moon in spring.

These with the rest, one and all, are to me miracles,

The whole referring, yet each distinct and in its place.

To me every hour of the light and dark is a miracle,

Every cubic inch of space is a miracle,

Every square yard of the surface of the earth is spread with miracles,

Every foot of the interior swarms with miracles.

—Walt Whitman

Giving the Moon

ON A CLEAR and beautiful night, a monk sat in front of his hut in the countryside, gazing at the full moon. Basking in the glow of the moon, the monk did not hear a thief creeping up behind him.

"Give me all you own!" cried the thief.

The monk replied, "My hut is empty. My only possessions are these ragged clothes. Come sit here with me. I am happy to share the beauty of the night sky with you."

The thief was not interested. Again he cried, "Give me all you own," and so the monk removed his clothes and handed them over. The thief tucked them under his arm and left.

Gazing up at the moon once more, shivering in the chill night air, the monk watched the thief make his way down the mountain. With a sigh he said to himself, "What a poor man! I wish I could give him this beautiful moon."

—A Zen story from Japan

The Creation

AND GOD stepped out on space,
And he looked around and said:
I'm lonely—
I'll make me a world.

And far as the eye of God could see
Darkness covered everything,
Blacker than a hundred midnights
Down in a cypress swamp.

Then God smiled,
And the light broke,
And the darkness rolled up on one side,
And the light stood shining on the other,
And God said: That's good!

Then God reached out and took the light in His hands,
And God rolled the light around in His hands
Until He made the sun;
And He set that sun a-blazing in the heavens.
And the light that was left from making the sun
God gathered it up in a shining ball
And flung it against the darkness,
Spangling the night with the moon and stars.
Then down between
The darkness and the light
He hurled the world;
And God said: That's good!

Then God himself stepped down—
And the sun was on His right hand,
And the moon was on His left;
The stars were clustered about His head,
And the earth was under His feet.
And God walked, and where He trod
His footsteps hollowed the valleys out
And bulged the mountains up.

Then He stopped and looked and saw
That the earth was hot and barren.
So God stepped over to the edge of the world
And He spat out the seven seas—
He batted His eyes, and the lightnings flashed—
He clapped His hands, and the thunders rolled—
And the waters above the earth came down,
The cooling waters came down.

Then the green grass sprouted,
And the little red flowers blossomed,
The pine tree pointed his finger to the sky,
And the oak spread out his arms,
The lakes cuddled down in the hollows of the ground,
And the rivers ran down to the sea;
And God smiled again,
And the rainbow appeared,
And curled itself around His shoulder.

Then God raised His arm and He waved His hand
Over the sea and over the land,
And He said: Bring forth! Bring forth!

And quicker than God could drop His hand,
Fishes and fowls
And beasts and birds
Swam the rivers and the seas,
Roamed the forests and the woods,
And split the air with their wings.
And God said: That's good!

Then God walked around,
And God looked around
On all that He had made.
He looked at His sun,
And He looked at His moon,
And He looked at His little stars;
He looked on His world
With all its living things,
And God said: I'm lonely still.

Then God sat down—
On the side of a hill where He could think;
By a deep, wide river He sat down;
With His head in His hands,
God thought and thought,
Till He thought: I'll make me a man!

Up from the bed of the river
God scooped the clay;
And by the bank of the river
He kneeled Him down;
And there the great God Almighty
Who lit the sun and fixed it in the sky,

Who flung the stars to the most far corner of the night,
Who rounded the earth in the middle of His hand;
This Great God,
Like a mammy bending over her baby,
Kneeled down in the dust
Toiling over a lump of clay
Till He shaped it in His own image;

Then into it He blew the breath of life,
And man became a living soul.
Amen. Amen.

—*James Weldon Johnson*

9.

I can make a difference

by working together with others.

Drops that gather one by one finally become a sea.

—*Persian proverb*

Heaven and Hell

A CURIOUS MAN once asked to visit heaven and hell. Expecting hell to be a terrible, frightening place, he was amazed to find people seated around a lovely banquet table. The table was piled high with every delicious thing one could possibly want. The man thought, *Perhaps hell is not so bad after all.*

Looking closely, however, he noticed that everyone at the table was miserable.

They were starving, because, although there was a mountain of food before them, they had been given three-foot-long chopsticks. There was no way to carry the food to their mouths with such long chopsticks, and so no one could eat a bite.

The man was then taken to heaven. To his surprise, he found the exact same situation as he had seen in hell. People were gathered around a banquet table piled with food. All the diners held a pair of three-foot-long chopsticks in their hands. But here in heaven, everyone was happily eating the delicious food, for the residents of heaven were using their extra-long chopsticks to feed one another.

—A tale from China

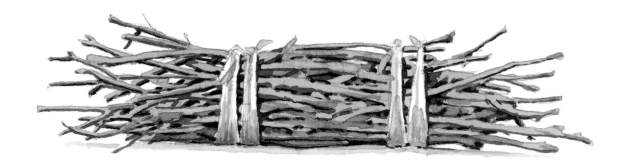

The Bundle of Sticks

DURING A TIME of war and famine, life was hard for all. One family of five sons made life even more difficult by fighting among themselves constantly. One day their father grew tired of their bickering. He spoke to them, asking, "When people around us are dying in battle and hunger, why must you act in such a way? Why can't you get along?" His words seemed to have no effect, so he instructed his eldest son to collect a bundle of sticks.

The eldest son did as he was asked and brought the bundle to his father. "Now break the sticks," his father commanded. The son, though strong, could not break the bundle. The second son tried and failed, as did the third and the fourth. When it was his turn, the fifth son untied the bundle and pulled out a single stick.

"Father," he said, "I know why you asked us to break this bundle. When we fight among ourselves, we are like this single stem"—and he snapped the stick in two—"and break easily. But when we stick together, we are impossible to defeat."

The father was happy to have raised such a wise son, and asked the older brothers to listen to him.

—Aesop

The Parts of the House Argue

HIGH UP in a nipa palm tree house, a large and quarrelsome family once lived. Not a day passed in the tree house without a disagreement of some kind. One day the family members began to quarrel about who was the most important member of the family. Soon the parts of the house began to argue about the same topic.

"I am the most important part," said one of the poles that held the house high off the ground. "I was the first pole driven into the ground. All the rest of you came after me."

The other poles disagreed. "Without us," one of them said, "you wouldn't be able to hold the house off the ground."

As the poles argued, the floor supports chimed in, "No one would care about the poles if we weren't here to hold you together!"

The cross supports called out, "Without us, you would all wobble and sag!"

The floor rumbled, "Without me, there's no reason for the rest of you!"

The bamboo walls rattled, "We make the rooms, and without rooms, this wouldn't even be a house!"

The roof beams and the ceiling and the palm leaf roof quarreled bitterly over which of them was the most important until, all at once, the many parts of the house realized that there was no way to win the argument, for each part was equally important. With one great breath the parts of the house sighed, "None is important without the other," and at that moment, the family members ceased quarreling as well. From that moment, the family lived together in peace.

—A tale from the Philippines

Swimmy

A HAPPY SCHOOL of little fish lived in a corner of the sea somewhere. They were all red. Only one of them was as black as a mussel shell. He swam faster than his brothers and sisters. His name was Swimmy.

One bad day a tuna fish, swift, fierce and very hungry, came darting through the waves. In one gulp he swallowed all the little red fish. Only Swimmy escaped.

He swam away in the deep wet world. He was scared, lonely and very sad.

But the sea was full of wonderful creatures, and as he swam from marvel to marvel Swimmy was happy again.

He saw a medusa made of rainbow jelly . . . a lobster, who walked about like a water-moving machine . . . strange fish, pulled by an invisible thread . . . a forest of seaweeds growing from sugar-candy rocks . . . an eel whose tail was almost too far away to remember . . . and sea anemones, who looked like pink palm trees swaying in the wind.

Then, hidden in the dark shade of rocks and weeds, he saw a school of little fish, just like his own.

"Let's go and swim and play and SEE things!" he said happily.

"We can't," said the little red fish. "The big fish will eat us all."

"But you can't just lie there," said Swimmy. "We must THINK of something."

Swimmy thought and thought and thought.

Then suddenly he said, "I have it! We are going to swim all together like the biggest fish in the sea!"

He taught them to swim close together, each in his own place, and when they had learned to swim like one giant fish, he said, "I'll be the eye."

And so they swam in the cool morning water and in the midday sun and chased the big fish away.

—*Leo Lionni*

Let us put our minds together and see what life
we can make for our children.

—*Sitting Bull*

Dr. George Washington Carver

10.

I can make a difference

by being compassionate and kind.

My religion is very simple. My religion is kindness.

—*The Dalai Lama*

EXCERPT FROM A letter from the great scientist *George Washington Carver* to the Tuskegee class of 1922, dated January 9, 1922

As your father . . . I hope . . . each one of my children will rise to the full height of your possibilities, which means the possession of these eight cardinal virtues which constitutes a lady or a gentleman.

1st. Be clean both inside and outside.

2nd. Who neither looks up to the rich or down on the poor.

3rd. Who loses, if needs be, without squealing.

4th. Who wins without bragging.

5th. Who is always considerate of women, children and old people.

6th. Who is too brave to lie.

7th. Who is too generous to cheat.

8th. Who takes his share of the world and lets other people have theirs.

May God help you to carry out these eight cardinal virtues and peace and prosperity be yours through life.

Lovingly yours,
G. W. Carver

The Month of March

IN ITALY, long ago, there lived two brothers. The elder, Cianne, was as rich as any-one in the land. The younger, Lise, was poor. Although he was rich in material things, Cianne was poor in spirit, and he refused to give Lise as much as a single coin on which to live. As a result, Lise set off to make his fortune on his own.

After walking all day, a tired, wet, and cold Lise stopped at a humble inn. Inside he found twelve young men sitting around a blazing fire. Taking pity on Lise, they took him in out of the rainy and cold March night. Lise was happy to be inside, and as he warmed his hands, one of the young men watched him closely, with an annoyed look on his face. "What do you think of this weather?" he asked gruffly.

Lise was a thoughtful young man, and so he replied, "I think every month has a job to do, but men, being human, always want what they don't have. In the win-ter we complain about the cold, and in the summer we complain about the heat. If the months didn't do their duties, nature would be turned upside down. I say let us leave heaven to its course, and each month to its job."

The young man's cross expression brightened a little, but he continued in a 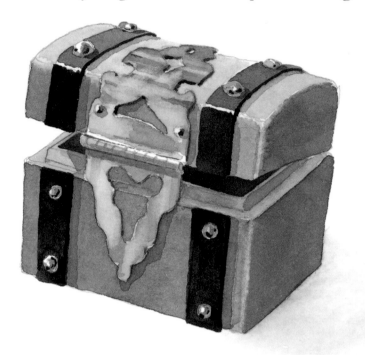 rough voice: "Even so, you can't deny that March is a particularly awful month, with its cold rain and frost and even snow."

Lise did not agree. "We must appreciate March as the gateway to spring and all its bounty. Without March, we would not have the grass and apple blossoms and young flowers of April and May. March starts all life growing again, and for that, I appreciate it."

With that, the young man's face creased into a smile, for he was March, and the other eleven youths around the fire were his brothers. He was so grateful to Lise for seeing the good in him rather than the bad that he decided to reward him. March gave Lise a tiny box with the instruction that, should he ever want for something, he had only to ask for it and open the box. Lise thanked him, and they all went to sleep for the night.

Early the next morning, Lise continued his journey. It was a cold and snowy day, and so, after a tiring morning of walking through the snow, he opened the box and wished for a carriage. Instantly a carriage appeared. When he wished for new clothes, they appeared as well. Satisfied that this box would provide him with all that he would need, Lise set out for home again.

He called on his brother, who was amazed at the things Lise had acquired. Lise explained about his trip and his visit with the twelve young men. He told Cianne of the box that March gave him, but said nothing of their conversation.

The next day Cianne hurried to the inn, anxious to get a magic box for himself. At the inn, all was as Lise had described; the twelve young men were sitting around the fire. When the cross man asked Cianne the same question about the month of March, Cianne, who was still cold and wet from his journey, said, "March is the worst month of the year! I wish it could be dropped from the calendar."

March managed to control his anger and said nothing. The next morning, when Cianne was about to leave, March presented him with a whip and said, "Whenever you wish for something, say, 'Whip, give me a hundred,' and you shall receive your reward." Cianne was very pleased, for he felt that a whip was bound to be at least as generous as the box that his brother had been given.

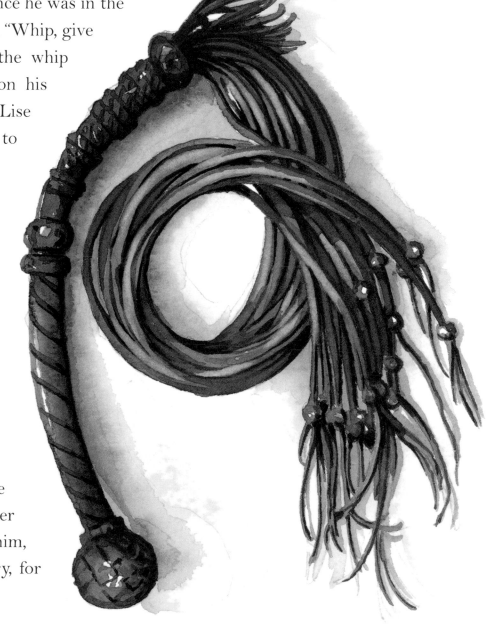

He hurried home, and once he was in the privacy of his room, he said, "Whip, give me a hundred." At once the whip commenced striking him on his legs, his back, and his face. Lise heard his cries and rushed to Cianne's room.

Cianne told him the story of how he came to have the whip. When he was through, Lise said, "You deserve what you got, for your cruel words and greedy nature have hurt many people. You should watch what you say, for you never know whom you may hurt with your words." But when he saw how dejected his brother looked, Lise took pity on him, and said, "But do not worry, for my box will provide enough for both of us, and I am happy to share. Let's forget the past and start again."

Cianne learned his lesson, for from that day on, he always spoke well of everyone, and his heart was full of love for all humankind.

—*An Italian fairy tale*

The Frog Prince

A LONG TIME AGO, there was a young princess who lived with her father the king. On a warm spring day, the princess sat by a well and amused herself bouncing a golden ball. She did this for hours, until the ball took an odd bounce and landed with a splash in the well. The princess began to cry, for she loved her ball, and there was no way that she could fetch it from the deep water of the well.

To her astonishment, a deep voice rumbled up from the depths of the well. "Why are you crying?" it asked. The princess called out that her ball had fallen into the well. Above the edge of the well, a large green frog appeared. It said, "If I return your ball to you, will you give me anything I want?"

"I will," replied the princess.

The frog did not want jewels or gold. He wanted only one thing: "I want to be your friend."

81

Without thinking, for she wanted her ball back, the princess agreed, and the frog retrieved her ball. Happy to have her ball back, the princess skipped away with only a brief nod of thanks to the frog.

That night at dinner, an anxious footman whispered in the king's ear, "There's a frog at the door, and he wishes to speak to the princess." The king was a jolly man, and he thought this was quite funny. When the princess told him the story, however, and described her promise to the frog, his smile faded. He was not only jolly, he was just, and the king explained to the princess that she must keep her word. The frog was brought to the table and a place was laid for him.

After dinner, the princess and the frog went to her room to play. When it was time for bed, the frog jumped up on the princess's fluffy bed. The princess was not happy. "You are a fat and slimy frog," she said, "and you'll ruin my bed. You cannot sleep on it."

With that the frog began to weep. "All I wanted," he whispered between sobs, "was to be your friend. But you think I am fat and slimy. You aren't my friend at all."

The princess took pity on the frog. "Oh, frog, what shall we do with you?" she said, and gave him a kiss.

In a flash, the frog turned into a sturdy young prince with bright eyes and a brilliant smile. He explained that a witch had cast a spell on him that could only be undone by the kiss of a beautiful girl. The princess and her good heart had released him from the spell.

The princess and her prince fell in love and were married. They lived lives of great happiness together, full of kindness to all, even those who seemed least deserving of it.

—*The Brothers Grimm*

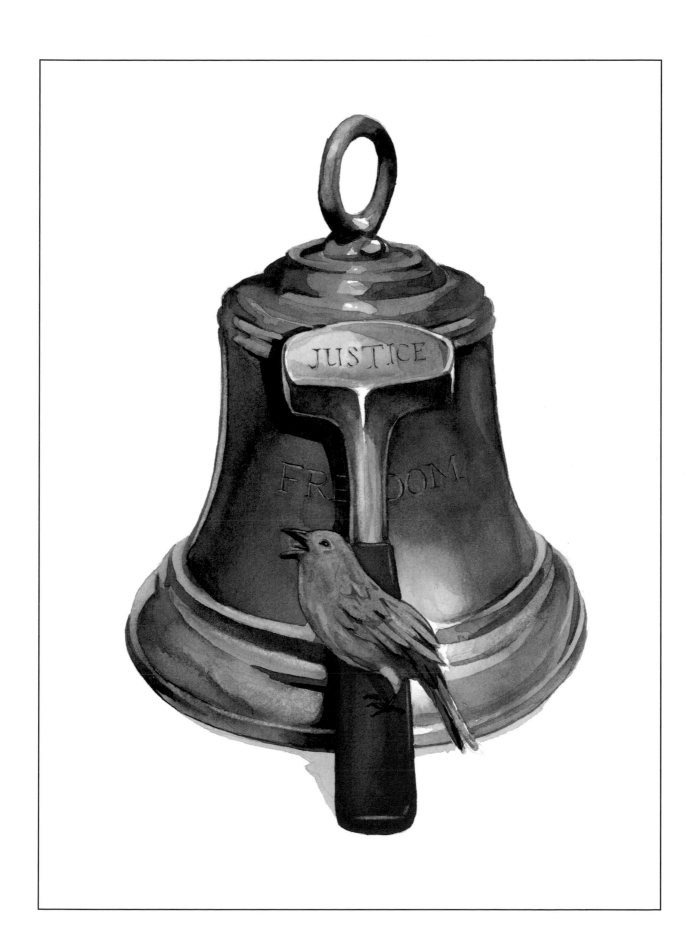

If I Had a Hammer

Words and Music:
Lee Hays and Pete Seeger

Nonviolence is the weapon of the strong.

—*Mahatma Gandhi*

We shall find peace. We shall hear the angels, we shall see the sky sparkling with diamonds.

—*Anton Pavlovich Chekhov*

Mother Teresa

12.

I can make a difference

by being faithful and struggling

for what I believe.

God has not called me to be successful. He has called me to be faithful.

—*Mother Teresa*

The more unpropitious the situation in which we demonstrate hope, the deeper the hope is. [Hope is] not the conviction that something will turn out well, but the certainty that something makes sense regardless of how it turns out. It is also this hope, above all, which gives us the strength to live and continually to try new things, even in conditions that seem as hopeless as ours do, here and now.

—*Václav Havel*

King Solomon's Ring

Of all King Solomon's servants, the bravest and most faithful was Benaiah, the captain of the guard. He had been the king's companion in the fabulous adventures of his earlier days and more than once had saved his master's life. He had never failed in any task that Solomon had set him.

This, indeed, was his only boast; for Benaiah was a man of action, not fond of talking. When he was not on duty guarding the king, he would sit among the courtiers so silent that they made the mistake of thinking him dull. They would tease him; but Benaiah, sure of his place with the king, paid no attention to them.

Once, however, Solomon himself took part in a mischievous trick they were playing on his faithful follower. "Benaiah," he said one Sabbath evening early in spring, "you are fond of saying that you have never failed in any task for me."

Benaiah bowed respectfully. "That is my only boast, O King."

"Then let me put you to one more test. I want you to find me a certain wonderful ring, so that I can wear it at the Succoth festival. That will give you six months for the search."

"If the ring exists under heaven, my lord, you shall have it! But tell me, I pray, what makes it so precious?"

"It has magic powers," said the king. "If a happy man looks at it, he at once